La Jolla / 92037

Published by:
En Ville
San Diego, California

http://www.envillepublishing.com

Printed in Shanghai
July 2010

ISBN 978-0-578-05969-3

La Jolla / 92037

Olivier Dalle
Paul Burlingame

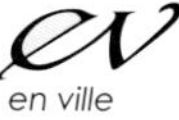

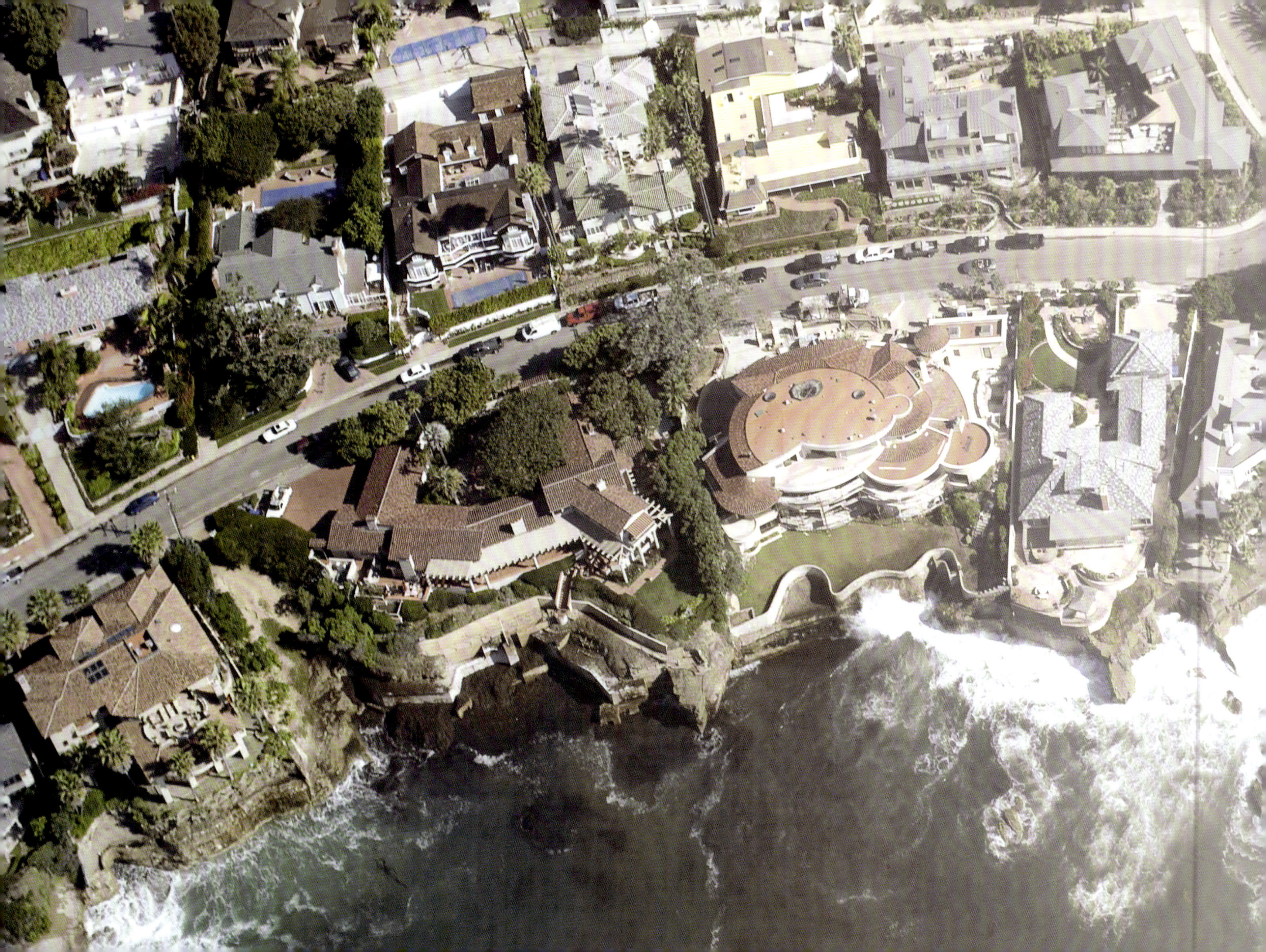

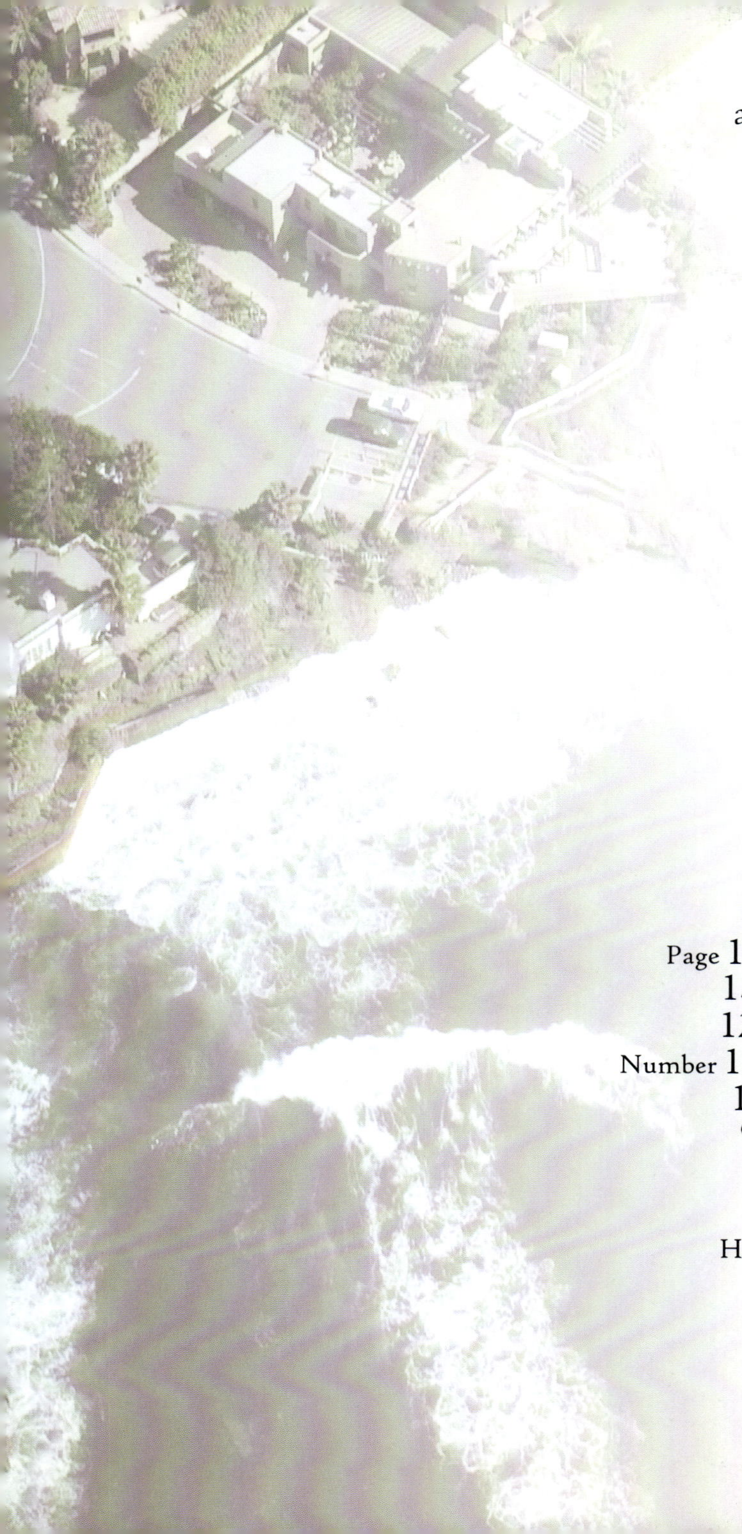

age 37

36 feet

35 years

34 customers

Tower 33

32 births

31 acres

Bus 30

29 feet

Score of 28

27 jello shots

26 swim caps

25 years

24 hours

23 dollars

22 employees

May 21st

20 feet

19 years old

18 again

17 people

16 chimes

15 minutes

Page 14

13 antique cars

12 million dollars

Number 11

10 legs

9 singers

8 hours

7 bookstores

Hole #6

5 beat poets

4 flavors

3 Nobel laureates

2 architects

1 surfer

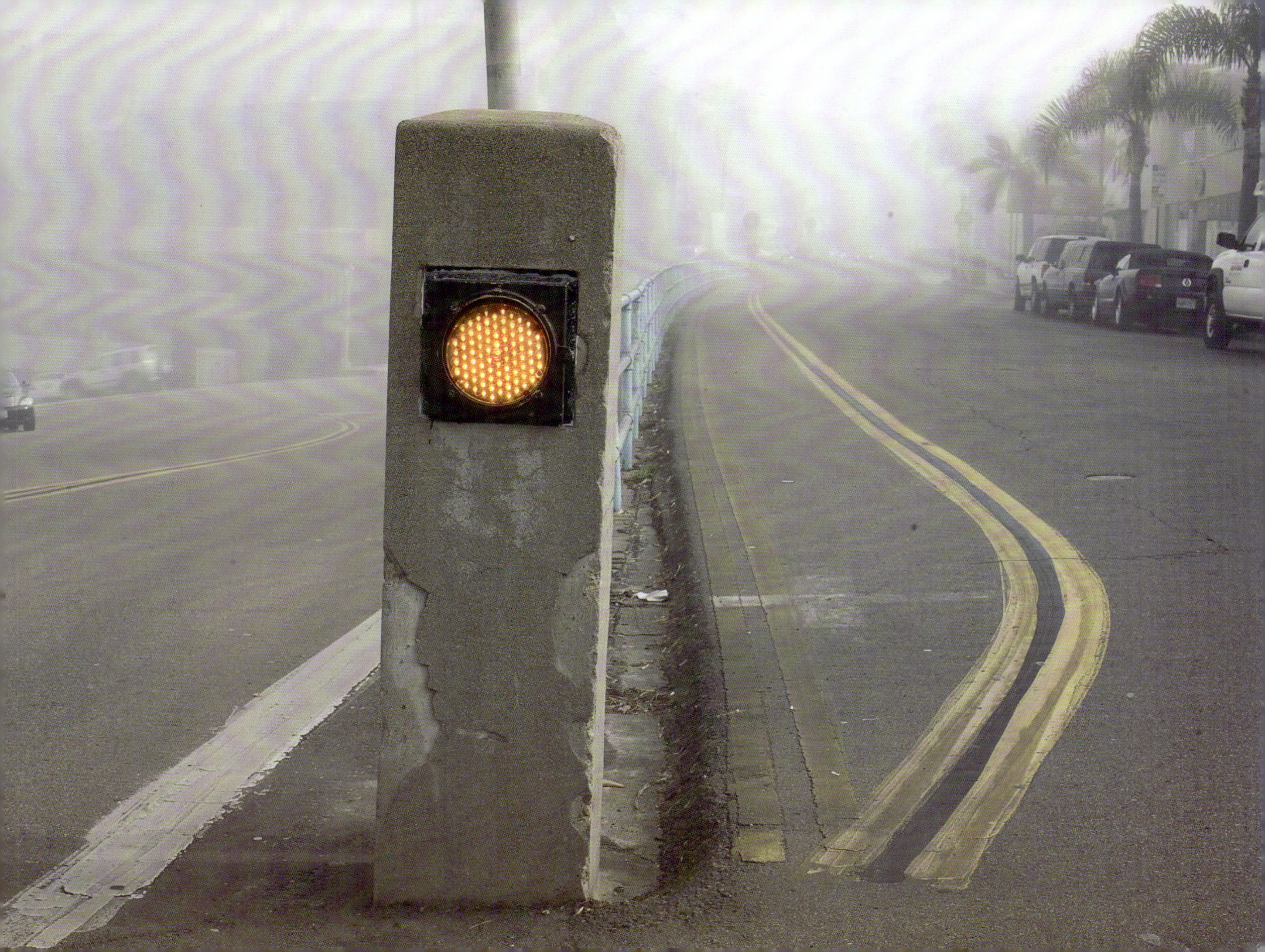

"We offer you a pleasant climate, balmy and invigorating sea-air, beautiful wild flowers, curious shells, smooth beaches, wonderful caves, sea mosses and ferns of rare beaches, ocean gold fish visible every day of the year, and occasional views of whales and vessels on the ocean."

So proclaimed the brochures advertising La Jolla Park in February of 1888. At the time, early tourists could count about eleven buildings in La Jolla: a hotel, hotel cottages, and a few houses. The exquisite scenery, the perfect climate – an annual average of 72° Fahrenheit without much variation throughout the year – and mostly the air, matchless, almost divine, were already here.

The stage has been set and it's awfully beautiful. Its shoreline bluffs are covered by ice plant as soft as carpet. The ocean is quiet today, and only small waves caress the sand. Almost nobody walks on the whimsically shaped beach. A lovely green square surrounded by a wall of stones, more ice plant, and a lush palm tree are unmistakably waiting for a ceremony of sorts. White seats are arranged around a graceful table covered with an immaculate white cloth. Empty and clean, every last one of them. Conventional stairs lead from the sea promenade to the waiting stretch of grass.

"La Jolla is a great place...for old people and their parents," said author Raymond Chandler, who lived in the neighborhood several decades ago. However, despite the luxurious Casa de Mañana retirement complex housing many happy retirees nearby, times are changing. Men living in the zip code today average *37* years old, which is younger than Chandler was when he wrote this. A heavy truck slowly trundles by, interrupting pleasant conversations and treating its driver to a long stretch of beautiful scenery between deliveries.

On the grass above the impending ceremony, a large family has just reserved a table near a public grill. Soon a multicolored kite is fluttering over everybody, and after a while music starts up in the distance. Gradually it draws closer, trailed by a tiny crowd: a photographer, musicians, and elegantly dressed ladies and gentlemen of all shapes and sizes. Their smiles and laughter fill the air with new fervor and emotion, and the few passers-by slow their gaits, their curiosity piqued by the event to come. And it arrives at last: an antique car halts in front of the vast ocean and the door swings open to reveal a smiling lady, a little shy, a little ceremonious. Exit a small parade of characters, ready to go.

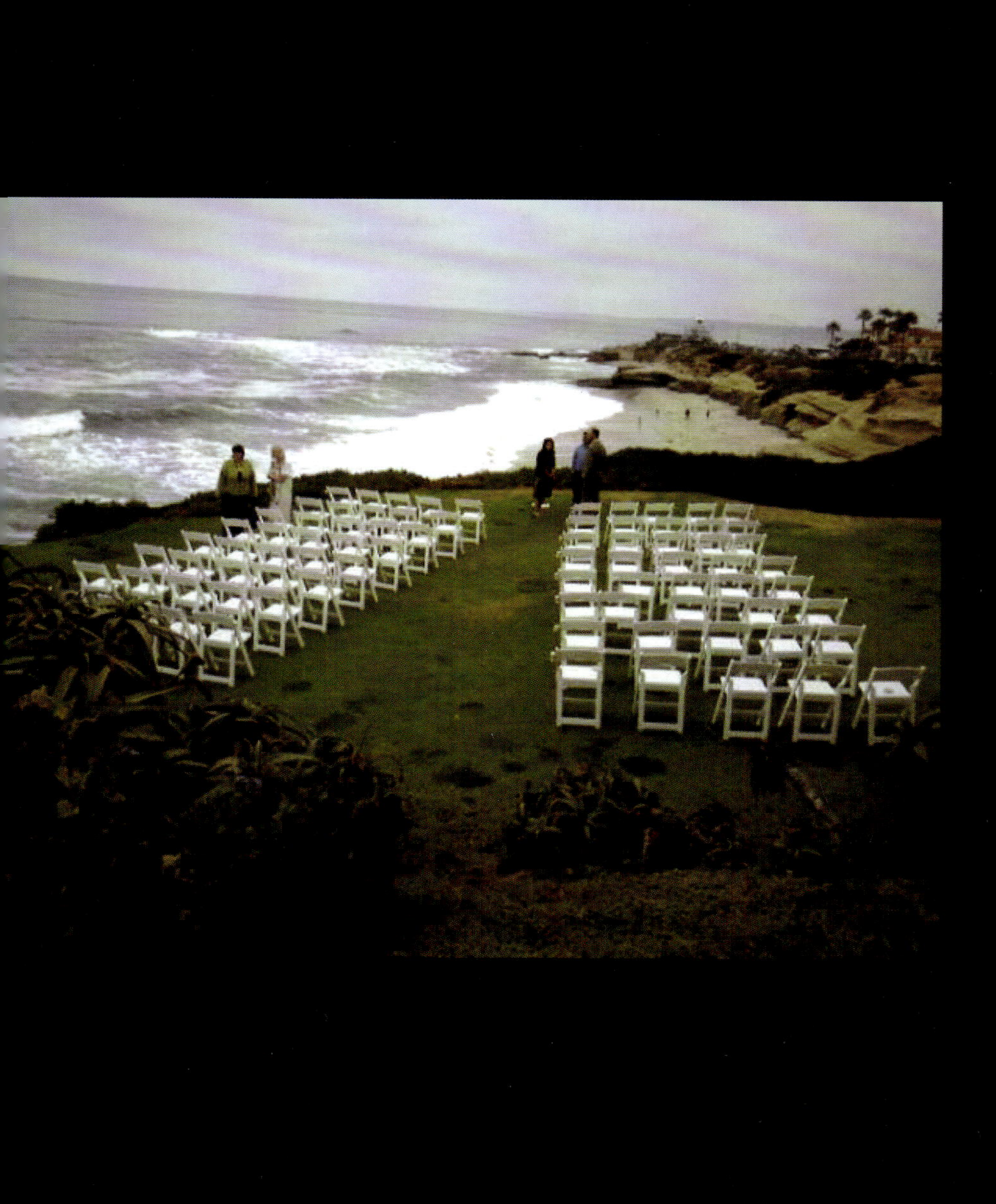

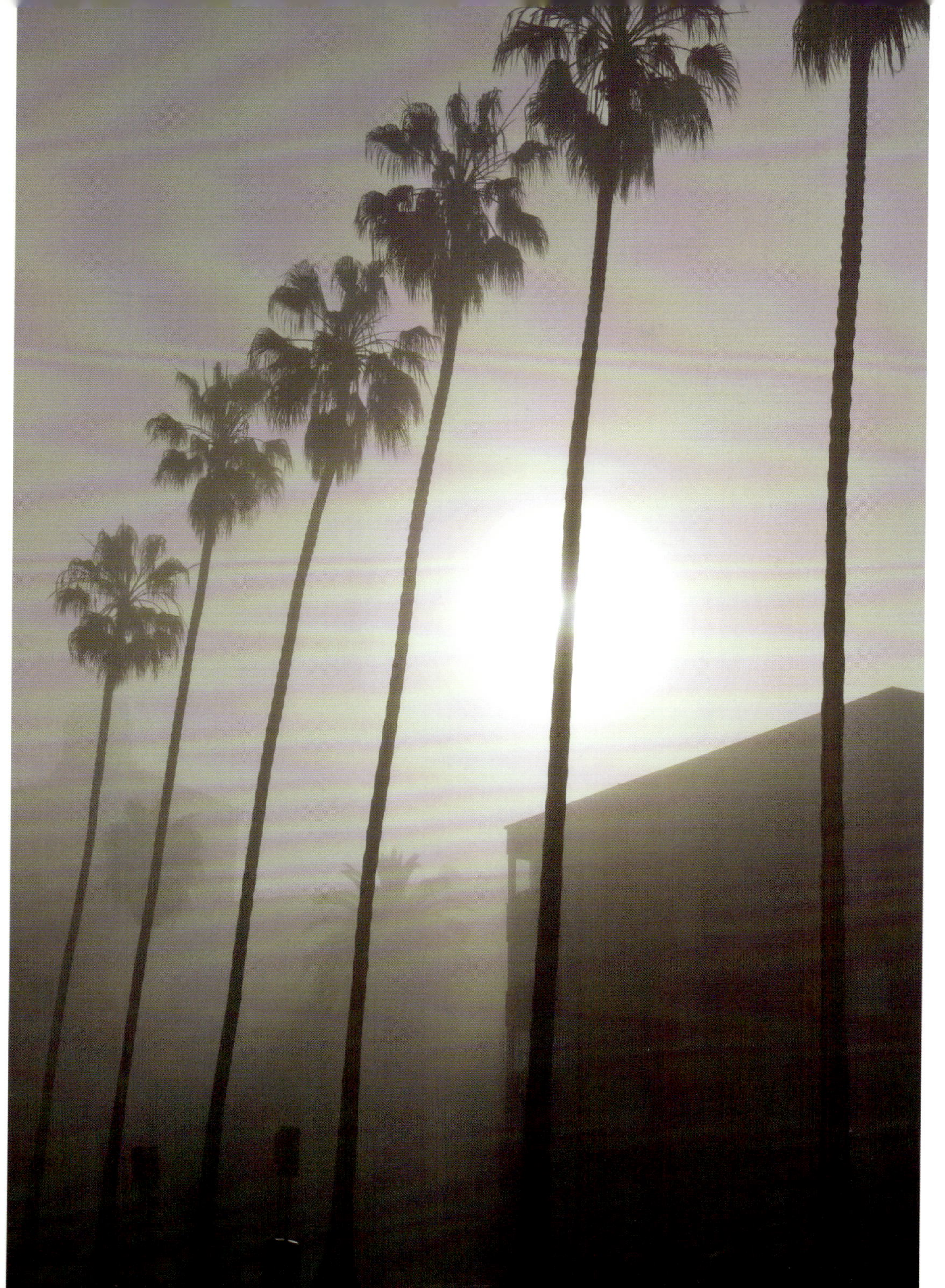

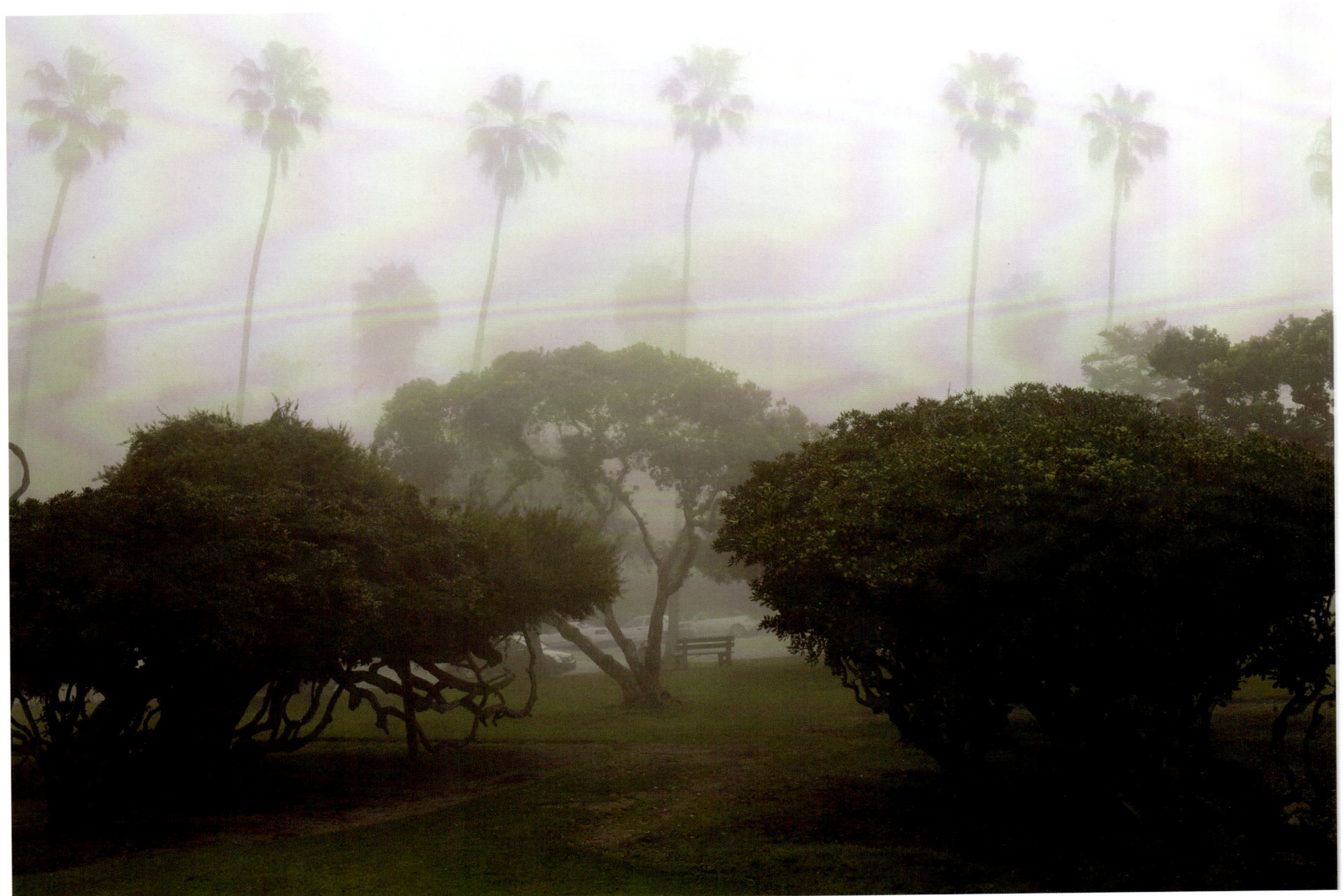

The climate in La Jolla stays about 72 degrees Fahrenheit all year round. However, in July, the high temperature is 80.80 degrees, and in January the low is 44.50 degrees. La Jolla receives about 11.97 inches of precipitation a year. Mount Soledad, a dominant landmark in the area, has an elevation of about 800 feet.

La Jolla is located 12 miles north of San Diego. The elevation is 110 feet. It contains 7 miles of coastline and 2 submarine canyons. It is home to the San Diego- La Jolla Underwater Park and Ecological Reserve, which encompasses 6,000 acres of ocean bottom and tidelands from La Jolla Cove to Shores. 52 different species of fish inhabit the area. Fishing is prohibited in a 533 acre zone within the park.

In some places near the city the ocean floor can reach depths of 600 feet.

The smells of wool and silk drifting from Aja Rugs at the corner of Girard and Prospect are pervasive even upon opening the door, but they intensify tenfold when one of the large rugs inside is unfolded in front of a potential customer. This one is a classic: a vast and symbolic hunting scene from the days of Cyrus the Great, founder of the Persian Empire, spread regally across the floor. Several of its pals hang on the walls, stretched out and proud to be on display, while the vast majority of others, rolled and piled on top of one another, wait for their turn to be considered. Their designs are unique and endless. Some feature a stylized forest, others a flower motif. Some consist mainly of Islamic patterns. One depicts a lavish Garden of Eden, lovebirds kissing in all four corners. They come mainly from Iran, but some also hail from Afghanistan, Pakistan, Turkey, Armenia, Nepal, or even Russia.

"How are you doing today?" asks a smiling and affable businessman, dressed in designer jeans and a long-sleeved shirt. His name is Adi Pourfard, and he, his partner Taba, and his sister

Baran are the affectionate guardians of these beloved rugs. Adi certainly looks like the personification of success and the American dream. Originally from Iran, where his father still lives and also sells rugs as Adi and his family have been doing for three generations now, he arrived in the US in the early 1980's. The confident smile is well justified: he now owns and runs four operational stores in La Jolla, in which he sells rugs that can some-times date back as far as the 17th century, go all the way up to $300,000 in price, and measure as many as 36 feet long by 25 feet wide.

Freshly arrived from Tehran last year, Adi's sister Baran, dressed in black, with long black hair and intense dark eyes, unfolds a blue, yellow and green 'Qālii' rug and then others marked with spirals and intricate motifs. They shine in the middle of Aja Rugs' white showroom, a prestigious and flashy place that looks almost as spacious and solemn as the entrance to an ancient Persian temple. Except it's all brand new, with large bay windows facing the Pacific Ocean.

Baran seems even more passionate than her brother about traditional Persian rugs and what they mean to the Iranian families who have owned them for generations. She talks about the time when soldiers in Cyrus great army used rugs to mount their horses more comfortably, and about how a traditional "mohtasham" can take seven years to complete his work. She also gently warns you that, in Iran, you shouldn't walk on a traditional Persian rug with your shoes on.

Later in the afternoon, after you've looked at, touched and smelled hundreds of rugs, after you've learned about their meanings and histories, you descend the stairs of the white palace. As you pass the terrace of the Living Room Café next door, you breathe in the apple-flavored narguileh traditionally smoked by Middle-Eastern men, and you're quietly wondering if you're ready to go check out a few more rugs on the other side of Prospect Avenue, at one of the other locations of the La Jolla Persian Rug Empire.

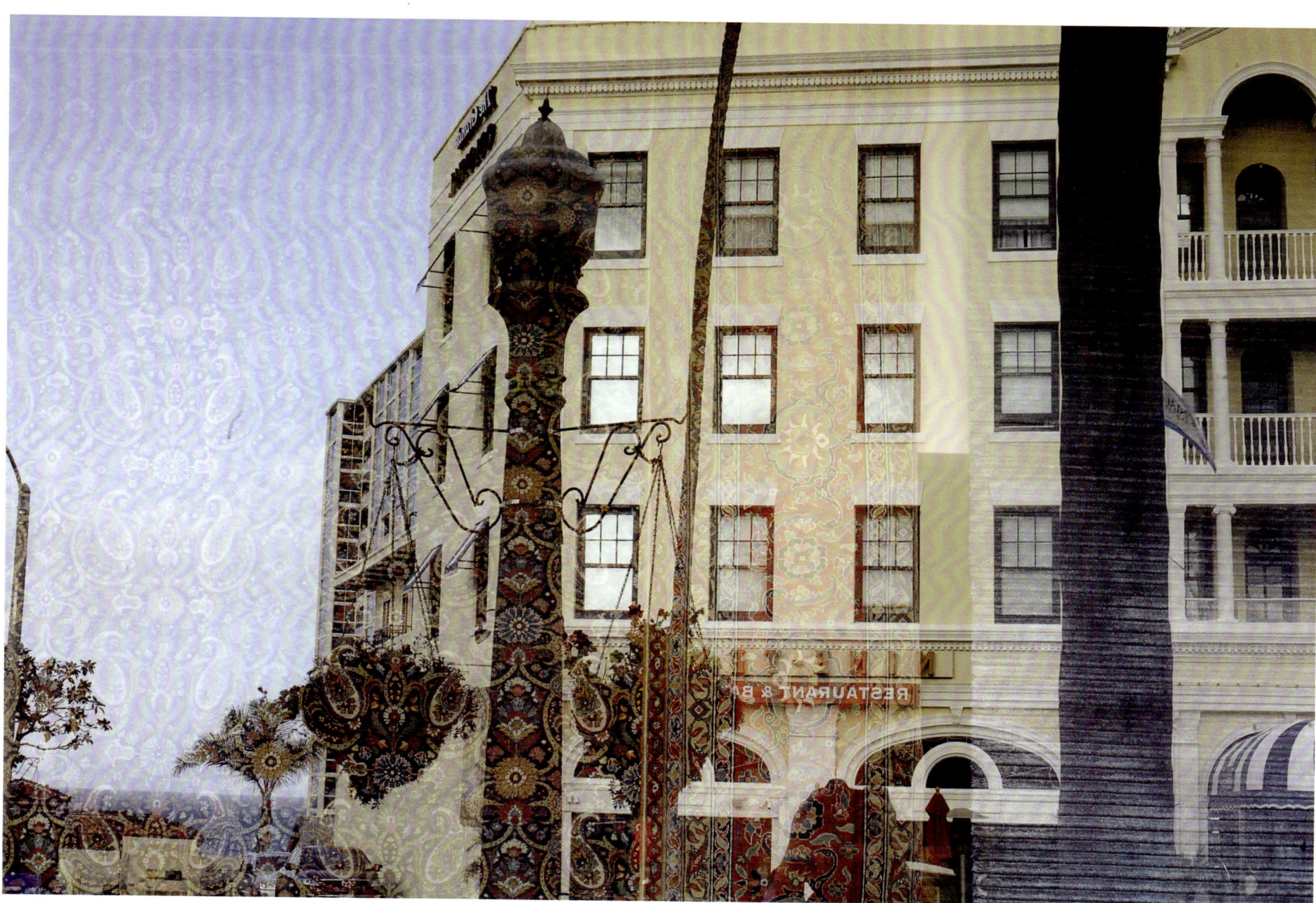

From the large bay window of their house perched on Mount Soledad, Robert Furstenthal and Françoise Farron take in the view of the whole North County coast and the orange sun's reflection on the calm ocean. It's a peaceful and soothing sight, unlike much of what happened before in their lives. Both were born in the 1920's in Vienna, Austria, each one growing up in a Viennese Jewish family with their parents and sisters. They were cousins and also childhood sweethearts, and their families, being close, visited each other often. Then, in 1938, the Nazis occupied Austria.

Robert and Françoise witnessed firsthand the "Kristallnacht" and the hardships that followed. Both of their fathers and one of Françoise's sisters were sent to Nazi concentration camps and died there. In February of 1939, Françoise escaped from Austria with her mother and arrived, shattered, in a small town in Switzerland. She had lost everything. All around her, people were celebrating *Mardi Gras*. Years went by, and in 1956 she resolved to move to America.

She arrived in New York aboard the Queen Elizabeth after a five-day crossing from Cherbourg, France.

Meanwhile, Robert received some unexpected help from a distant relative that his family had never heard of. A Mr. Brooks contacted his sister from America and offered to help them escape. Robert's father accepted on his son's behalf, and in 1940 Robert arrived in Halifax, Newfoundland and soon after that in New York City. There, the Jewish Refugee Center showed him a map of the US and asked him to pick a place. Robert picked San Francisco because it sounded nice, and set out across the country on a Trailways bus. For years, both Robert and Françoise lived their lives independently on opposite coasts of the country.

Finally, still preoccupied with thoughts of his childhood sweetheart even after all this time, Robert hired a detective to find Françoise in 1973. She was living in Boston at the time, doing bio-chemical research at Harvard Medical School, and responded to her long-lost admirer's greetings by sending him Austrian beef "Goulash" by mail. They arranged to meet at the San Francisco airport, fell in love all over again, and were wed one year later in California. After the wedding they arrived in La Jolla, where they're still living after 35 years, on the slopes of Mount Soledad. Long since retired, they now devote their lives to artistic endeavors, Françoise to painting, Robert to composing music, and both to watching the sun gently setting over the Pacific Ocean from their living room late each afternoon.

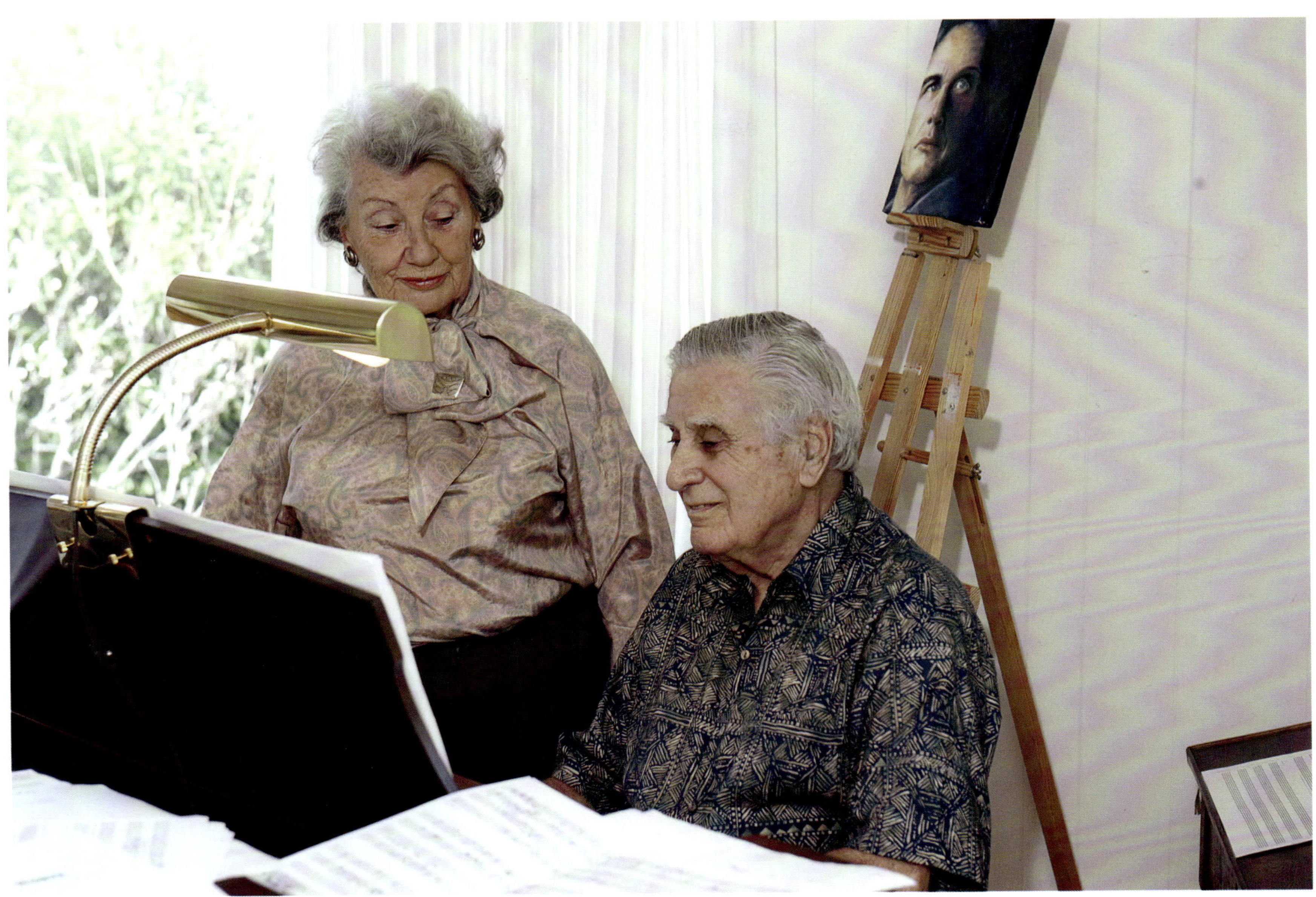

It's Friday morning at the Pannikin, and it's almost as crowded as a Sunday. Open since 6 a.m., it's been bustling with conversations about yesterday's rain and a mudslide that occurred somewhere in La Jolla for several hours already. The rich scent of warm brunches mixes with that of freshly brewed coffee; the sound of loud chatting with that of tinkling cups. Students strive to stay focused on their laptops and heavy textbooks, but can't resist looking around from time to time, mostly at other students who try to act as if they haven't noticed.

A group of quiet retirees talks politics in the shade of a gorgeous tree on the patio. A man dressed in a silky shirt and shorts with dark glasses and a raucous voice walks in and seems to know everybody. He greets some, asks others for the latest news, and nods perpetually as he deftly maneuvers his way toward the counter to order a drink. His pet, a French bulldog, waits patiently on the patio. A fluffy white poodle keeps him company. They both love it here: it's so laid-back, generous and unaffected... and the

café owners have left a bowl of fresh water out just for them.

Human locals love it, too. They come here all the time, settling down for hours in their favorite corners, feeling very much at home. Some come with their kids or their parrots; some come in their pajamas. Others are fresh from the ocean, their hair still wet and messy, their ears full of sand. Nobody seems to care. You can even speak strange languages: your amused neighbors will ask you where you're from, smile, and return to their omelets. Bushes and giant trees are everywhere. Although they're much older than the café, they look as though they've grown in among the wooden tables and benches.

Everybody seems to know the owners, either Amanda or her partner Renee, or both. They live a couple of blocks away. Renee, short haired with clear blue eyes, is here today. She's running around, greeting everyone she knows, everyone that is, serving customers when it becomes too

busy, checking the numbers. Locals in the queue gaze at the last vacant tables with longing. Between the shadowy patio and the warm interior with its fireplace, the art on the walls, and the giant chessboard, **34** customers are already seated today, sipping their drinks, eating their bagels, or petting their laptops. Amanda, blue-eyed like Renee but longhaired, hasn't arrived yet. She's roasting the coffee for all three Pannikins in San Diego, sometimes over 1,000 pounds per week. With any luck she'll also find time to chat with the band that's going to play tonight at 8 p.m., right here on the patio, under the gorgeous old tree.

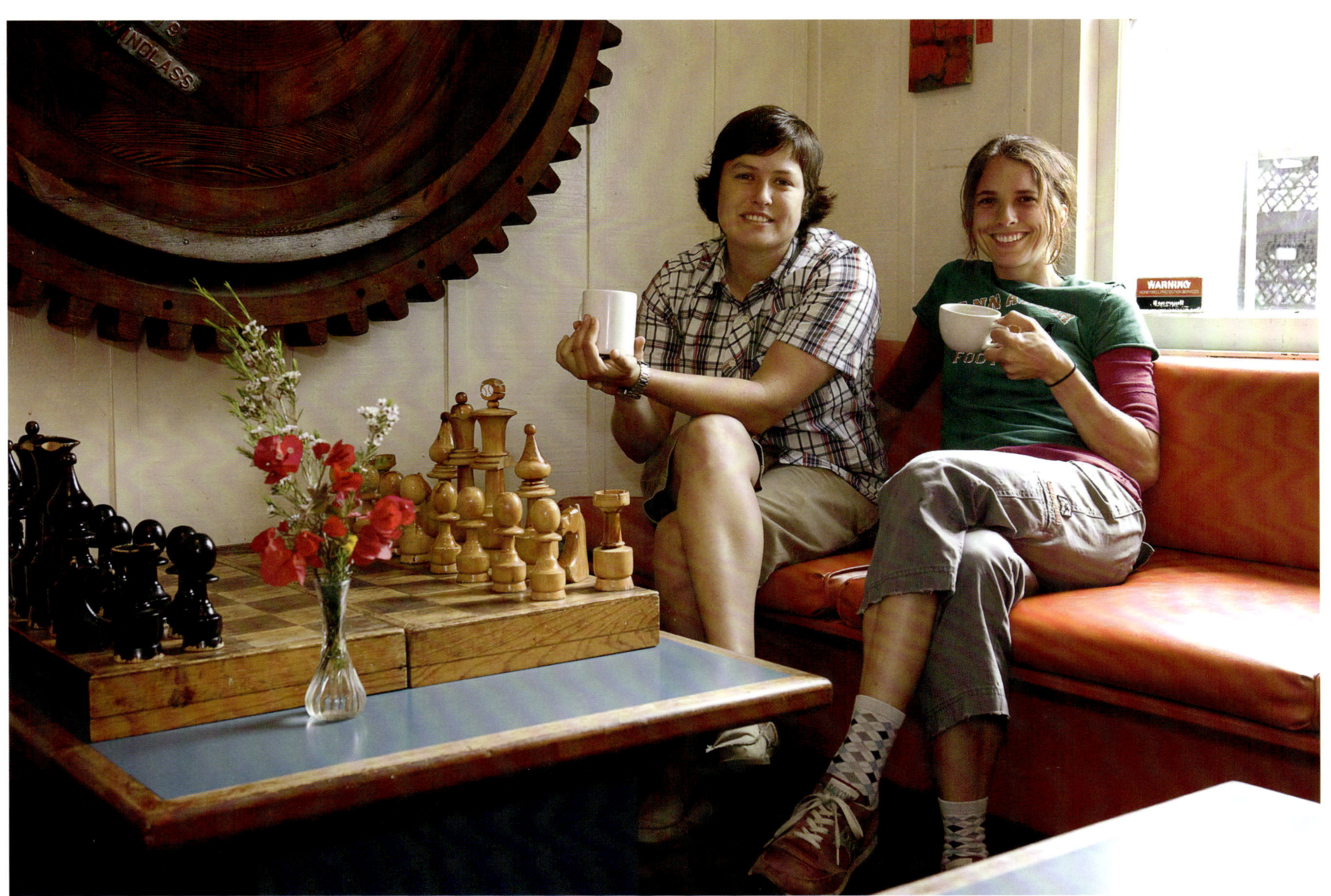

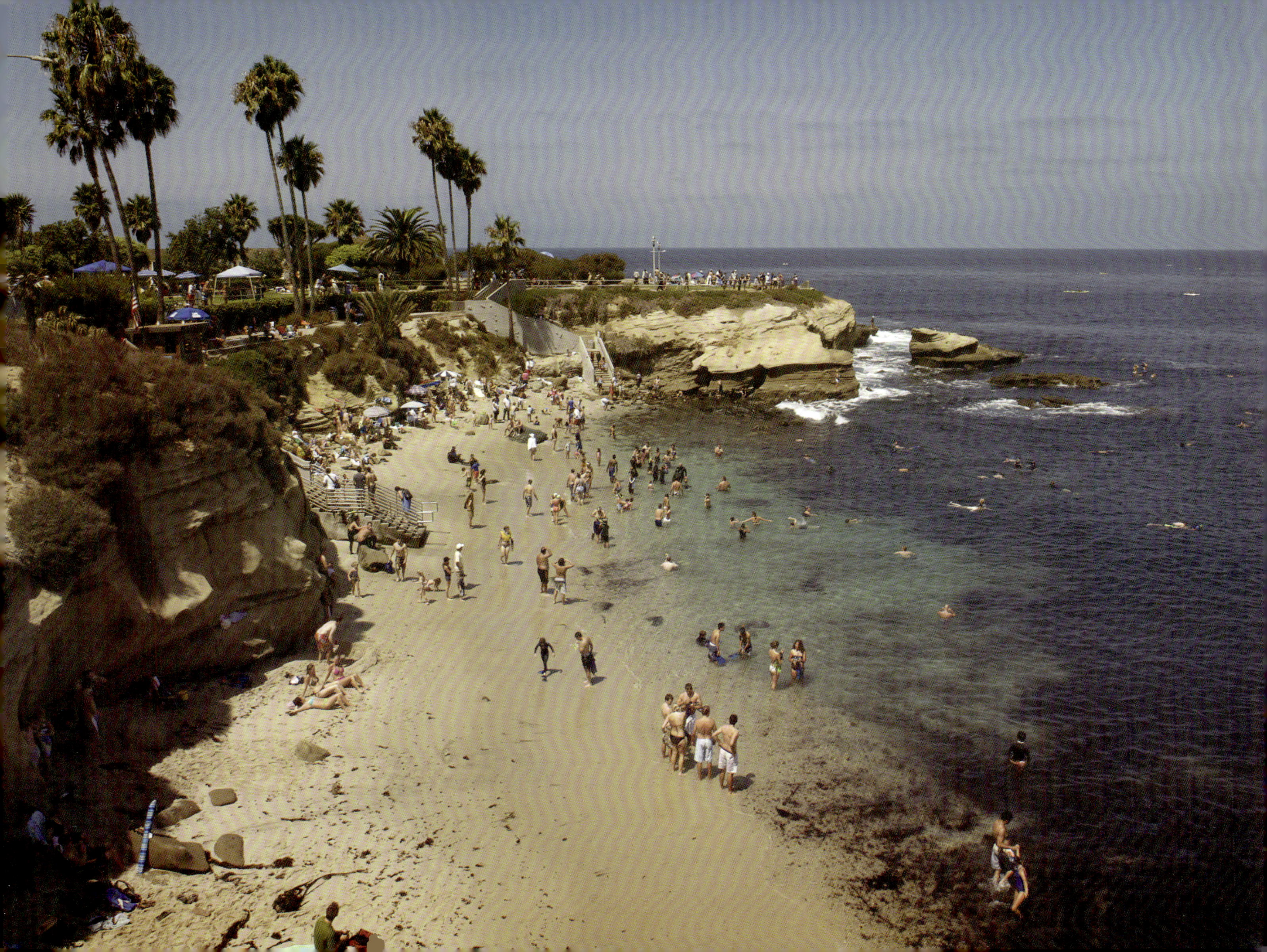

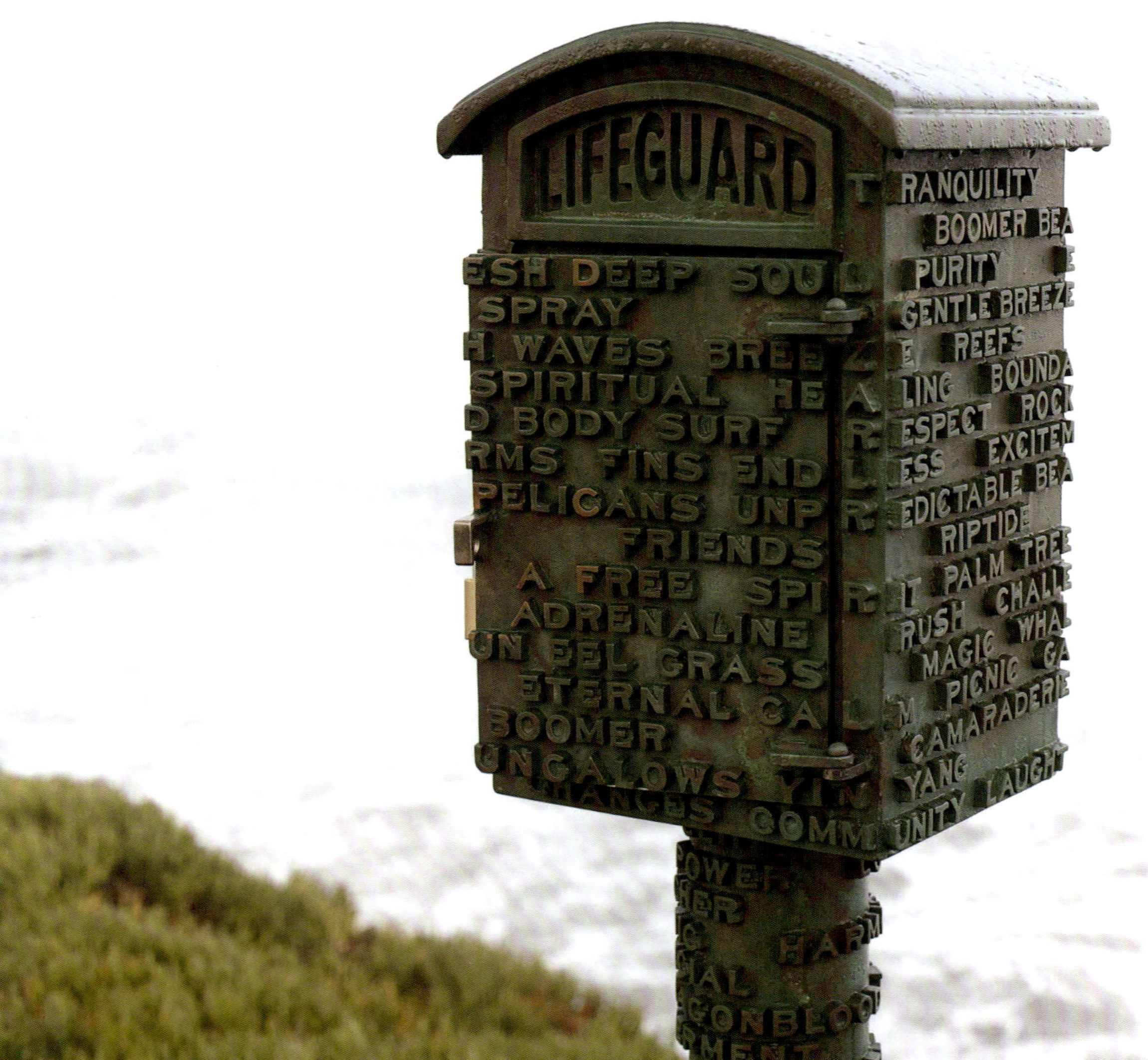

LIFEGUARD
TRANQUILITY
BOOMER BEA
PURITY
GENTLE BREEZE
REEFS
LING BOUNDA
ESPECT ROCK
ESS EXCITEM
EDICTABLE BEA
RIPTIDE
PALM TRE
RUSH CHALLE
MAGIC WHA
PICNIC GA
CAMARADERIE
YANG LAUGH
UNITY
ESH DEEP SOUL
SPRAY
WAVES BREEZ
SPIRITUAL HEA
BODY SURF
RMS FINS END
PELICANS UNPR
FRIENDS
A FREE SPIR
ADRENALINE
UN EEL GRASS
ETERNAL CA
BOOMER
UNGALOWS YIN
HANGES COMM
OWER
HER
HARM
AL
GONBLO
MENT

On yet another perfect summer morning in Windansea, two young, muscular and tanned lifeguards watch the calm crowd's every movement under a pure blue sky. Swimmers, joggers, sunbathers and surfers enjoy the rocks, the sand, the gentle breeze and the cool ocean's waters, which shift in color from clear turquoise-blue to a weed-like brown. The lifeguards smile before they speak, used to a measured pace in every-thing they do. They're not supposed to chat casually with outsiders when they're on duty, so they remain silent for a long time before answering people's questions, scanning the horizon from left to right and right to left with their steady eyes.

On very quiet days such as this one, it seems that there are no rescue operations to be had. But in the past 10 years in the city of San Diego, for an average beach attendance of 20,000,000 people a year, there were about 10,000 various rescues by lifeguards and 1 to 5 drownings. Without question the busiest area for the 40 or so lifeguards in La Jolla, whose ranks include about 10 women, is not Windansea or the Cove but the Shores, and the busiest time of the year for them is naturally the summer. On a 4th of July in La Jolla Shores, which draws more crowds than any other single day on the calendar, they sometimes conduct as many as 100 rescue operations. One of the taciturn life-guards breaks his silence long enough to estimate that on average they rescue about 20 people a week in Windansea during the summer, compared to about 100 a week at Shores. But today, the quiet crowd seems keen on staying on the safe side.

Meanwhile in La Jolla Shores, around Lifeguard tower *33*, the masses are less interested in caution. Here the beach is so crowded that most people don't notice the beautiful, thin layers of clouds appearing on the horizon. The smell of sunscreen saturates the air, and the lazy sound of crashing waves muffles the crowd's laughter and screams. Groups of girls in bikinis stretch out under the sun and gossip about handsome young men – lifeguards, maybe. But as for the lifeguards themselves, it's difficult to get a hold of them. Three or four dash by with walkie-talkies, making a beeline from the main lifeguard station with its loud microphone to a white pick-up truck piled high with rescue surfboards. Looking at the ocean where swimmers, surfers, boogie boarders and out-of-state tourists of all shapes and volumes mingle recklessly, it's not hard to believe the stats and under-stand the constant rush inside the main tower. As if to prove the point, a blond fellow with a moustache rushes out of it and hops into his rescue pick-up truck parked in the sand, careful to avoid half-naked bodies, towels and picnic food as he shifts it into gear. Someone has called for help, it seems, and he's gone in a flash, speeding north toward Scripps pier, leaving grooves in the sand behind him.

The number one political debate, the single most passionately discussed controversy in La Jolla, has to be the "seals issue." This dispute has been raging since the 70's, when the object of the controversy, a colony of about 200 harbor seals, wandered its way into what used to be known as the "children's pool" – the beautiful beach located in the heart of La Jolla that is famous for its calm waters and scenic pier. Things escalated when, a couple of decades later, the seals adopted the beach in large numbers, and swimmers began to desert it.

Harbor seal lovers and ecstatic tourists loved this development and flocked to the beach in large numbers to admire or sometimes to poke fun at the lazy mammals. However, other locals viewed the situation very differently. To them, the seals were party crashers, depriving them of their right to swim at one of the most beautiful beaches in La Jolla, which they now call "Casa Beach." Resolved not to give in without a fight, they often go swimming among the seals, making sure to disturb the invaders as much as possible, a secret smile hiding under their diving masks. Back on street level, seal supporters look on with outrage, rallying passers-by to their cause and shaking their large pro-seals banners even more intensely.

Unaware of the debate churning around them, the harbor seals themselves like to hang out in the sand by the sea wall, or in a rock caressed by the ocean waves, cooed at and admired by their more indulgent visitors. Seals can hold their breath under water for up to 30 minutes and dive as deep as 600 feet. However, in order to survive, each day they have to come out of the water onto dry land, where they spend 30 to 40 percent of their time. Their life expectancy ranges from 20 to 25 years, and the average duration of female pregnancy is, as with human mothers, about nine months.

But while the harbor seals live carefree lives, human swimmers, gathering at websites such as *friendsofthechildrenspool.com*, and friends of the seals, who can be found at *lajollaseals.com*, have not yet resolved their differences. From August 1998 to January 2008, 19 legal documents were filed in the ongoing struggle between the pro-seals faction and the pro-swimmers group. In 2004, a decision was made by the San Diego City Council to dredge the beach to encourage tidal flushing, but the issue is still on appeal. In 2006, the Council decided after vigorous debates to install a rope barrier to keep people from harrassing the seals during pupping season, from January to May. Meanwhile, life goes on. In 2007 there were **32** births reported among the seals at Casa Beach, and many more among the humans in the area.

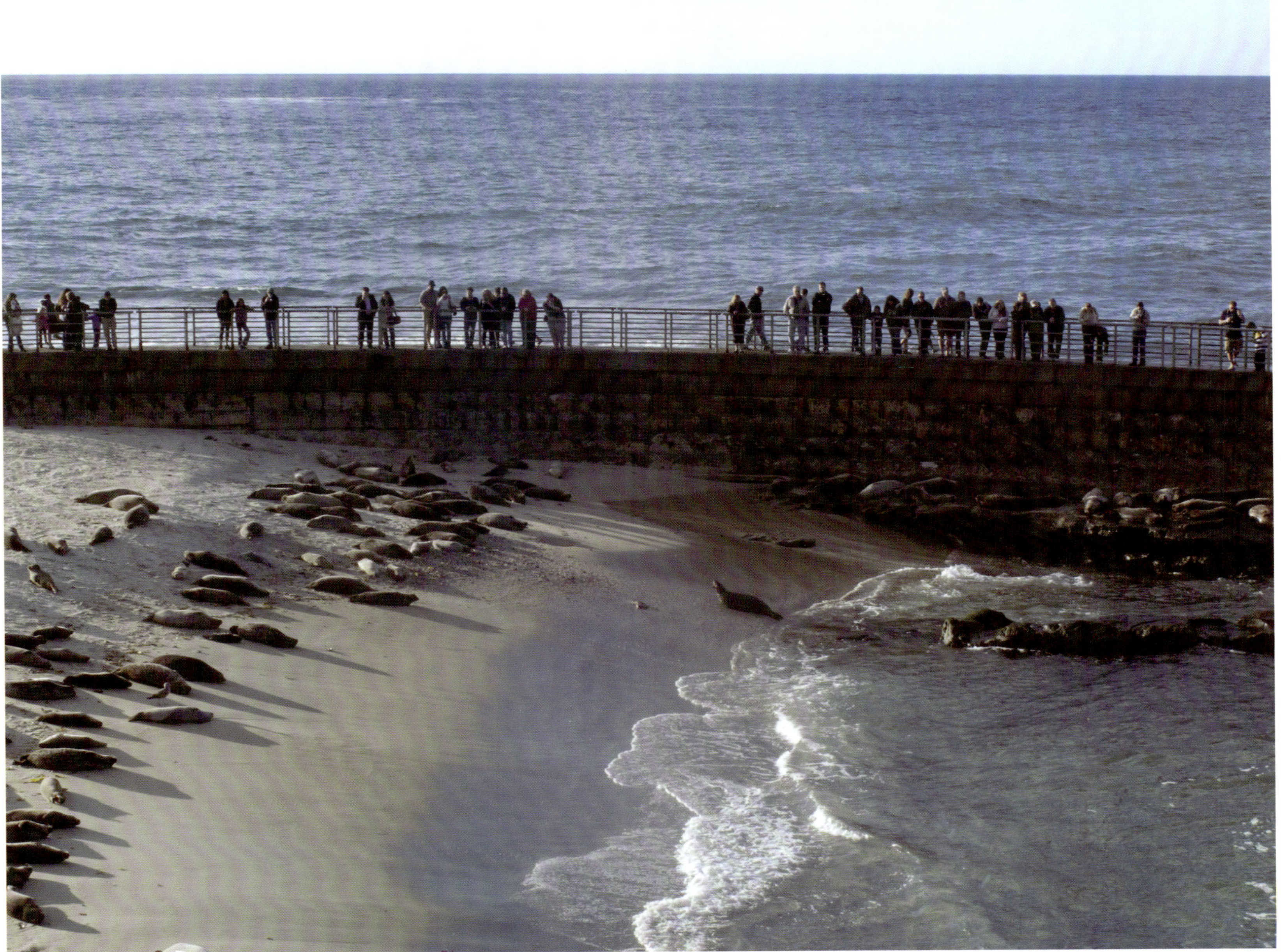

It's about 12 noon on Sunday, and the La Jolla farmers' market by the elementary school on Girard is already pulsing with sound. Near the entrance, about a dozen stands sell clothes, antiques, various accessories, and some art. At the heart of the market, independent farmers sell their products to happy locals. Georges, the older, gentle owner of Betty B's ranch, watches it all from behind his stand as he chats with a customer. He's here every Sunday, and he knows the place well.

Along the aisles of the flavorful, open-air market, beautiful tomatoes, zucchinis, spices, all types of salads, and an amazing variety of squash tempt passers-by. Confection squash and winter squash cost $2 a pound today, sunshine squash, $2.50, and mini squash, $5.99 a pound. Next to the usual medley of flowers, benches of aromatic herbs stretch out along the path, basil, sorrel, thyme, cilantro, rave, and arugula among their most popular attractions. The fruits are also appealing, their colors and shapes a natural tableau that's reminiscent of enchanting postcards. Further up the road, Hachiya persimmons vie for attention with Fuyu persimmons, and more flowers lie in ambush of unresisting customers at every turn. European mothers snap up things like Oroblanco grapefruits for 79 cents and elephant garlic at $8 a pound. A blue-haired clown smears face paint on a chubby-cheeked child. One woman stands indecisively over a display offering eight types of potatoes in yellow, white, red or black, of all sizes and shapes.

As he does every Sunday, Georges takes it all in, a tired, gentle smile on his face. He has been working alone on his Sedona ranch for *31* years, and times only seem to be getting harder for independent farmers like him. Of the 31 acres that make up his ranch, only 12 of them are planted right now. Georges sometimes waves to or smiles at a passing familiar face, but in general he spends more time sighing quietly to himself as the hours go by. A young couple buys Mexican *mole* and a *chilaquile* at the stand opposite his, kissing almost imperceptibly while two sweating women cook their lunch before their eyes. Further off in the market, Asian BBQ, Turkish *kebabs*, Greek *gyros*, French *crepes*, Italian ice-creams, smoothies, slushies, fresh squeezed orange juice and even fresh sugar cane juice are also available, though the steady stream of visitors at his neighbor's booth mark it as a popular choice. The sun is just starting its lingering afternoon descent as Georges wipes down his table. He casts his gaze over the crowd again: people buying food and drinks, fruits and veggies, picnicking on the grass, charmed one and all by the gentle brouhaha. Next Sunday, it will all begin again.

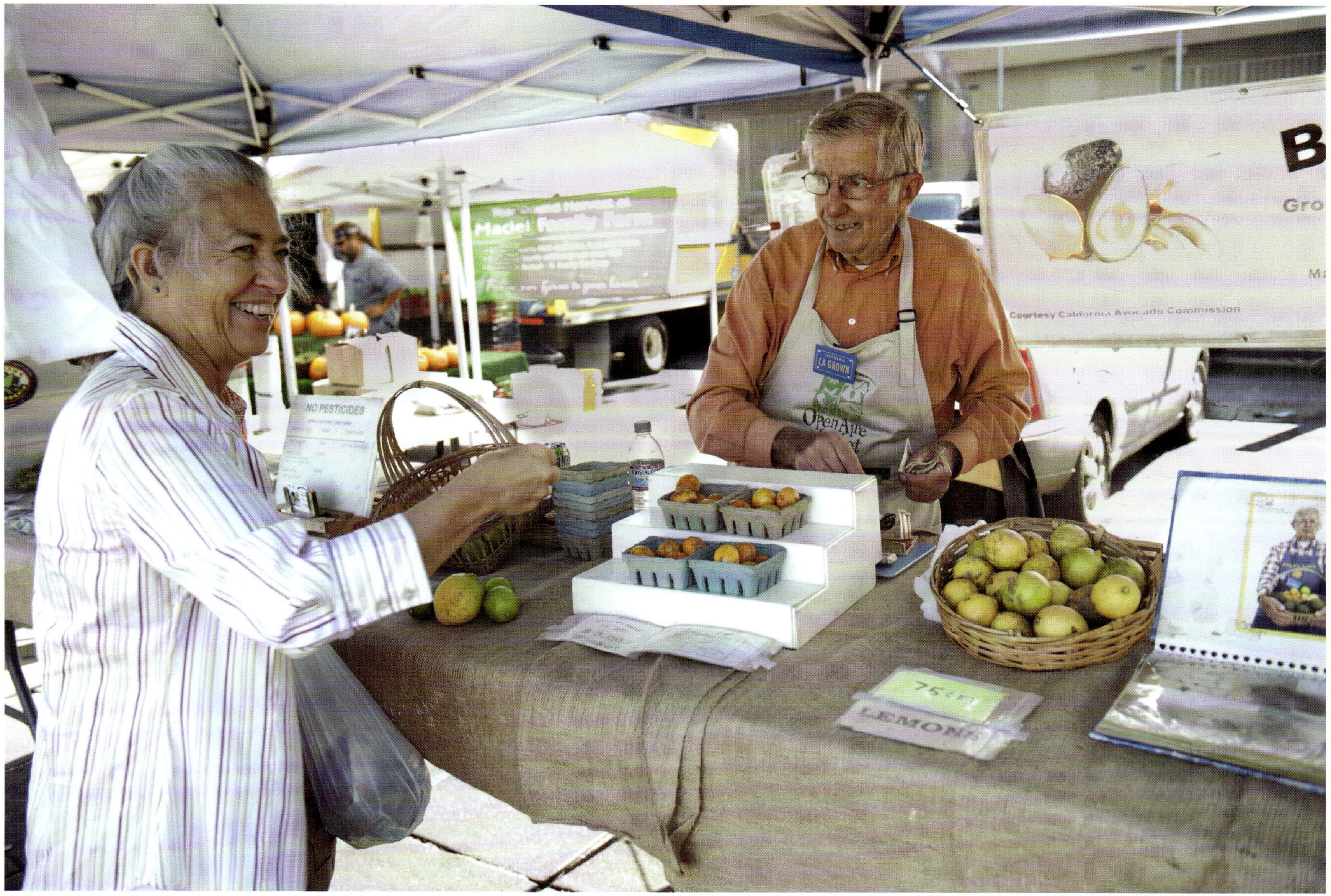

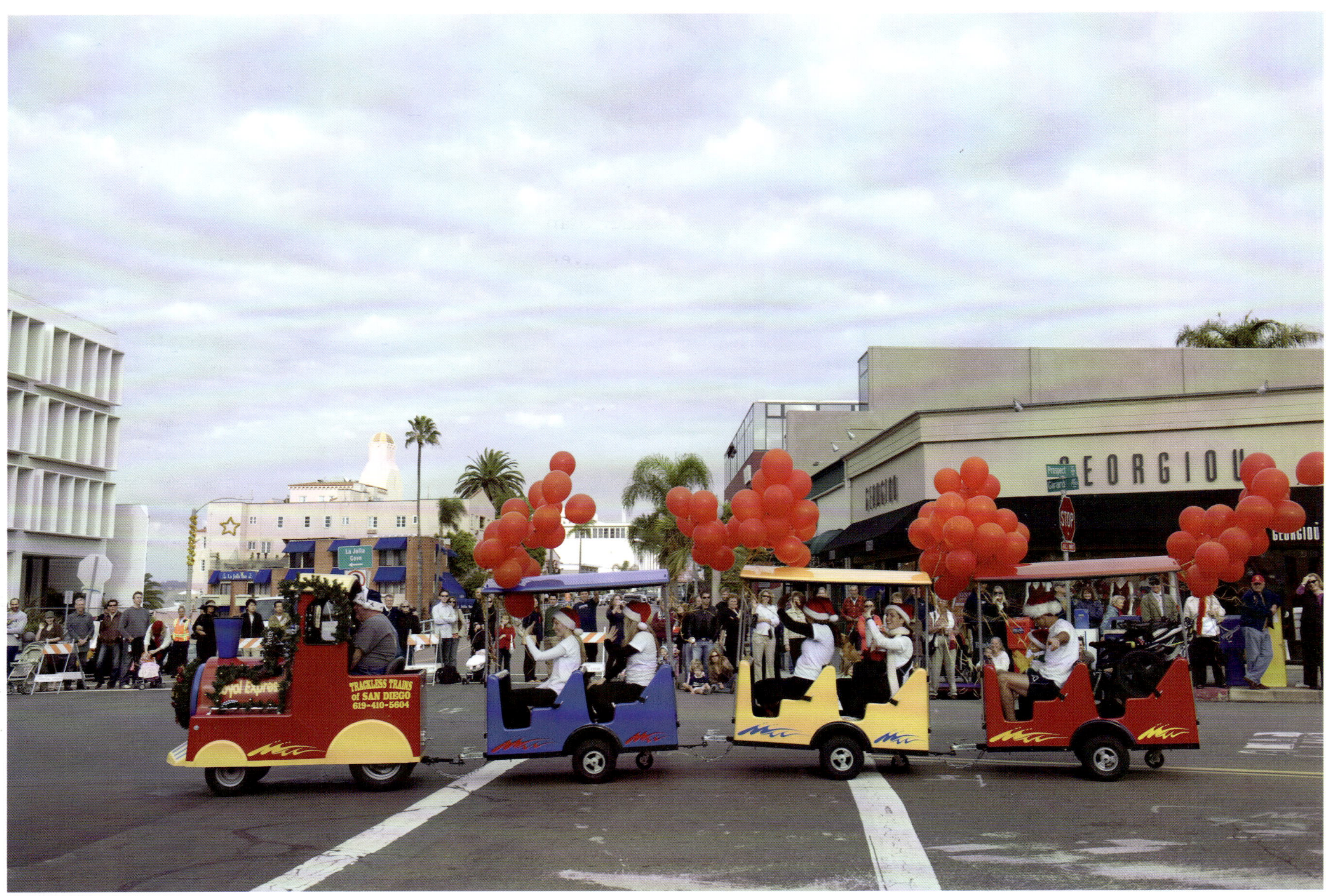
TRACKLESS TRAINS
of SAN DIEGO
619-410-5604
GEORGIOU
STOP

In 1900, 350 people lived in La Jolla.

By the end of World War I, the population had grown to 4,000. Many of the service members picked up and moved to La Jolla after World War II ended, and by 1960 there were more than 17,000 people living there. In 2000, there was an average of 2 people per household in any given 12.9 square miles of land.

Women are 2.5 years older than men on average.

There are 1,945 more women in La Jolla than men. In La Jolla, the median age is 37.1 years for men and 39.6 for women. By contrast, the average Californian is younger – only 33.3 years old. Today, there are around 44,000 people living in the zip code 92037.

6,676 of them are children. Among these youngsters, 6,300 of them are natural, 198 are adopted, and 178 are stepchildren. The population in La Jolla is now 3,317 people for every single sq. mile.

Luxurious German sedans, Italian sports cars and massive black SUVs typically compete for space in the streets of La Jolla. Locals and visitors alike ostentatiously park their jewel of an automobile, be it a shiny classic car or a brand-new beauty, in front of the restaurant, store or bank where they have their date, errand or meeting before merging smoothly back into the sea of expensive vehicles. It is difficult to imagine anything resembling public transportation ever venturing into this area and yet, what are these two people waiting for at the intersection of Girard and Silverado on this cloudy morning?

"Usually, they're on time," an older gentleman wearing a perfectly ironed shirt, a baseball cap, and white gloves tells a shy-looking Latina lady, who sits on one of the two metal benches without saying a word in reply. The strange creature arrives two minutes after, slightly fuming. There is a large number *30* on its forehead. It rumbles to a stop in front of the few passengers. The automatic door opens slowly. "I told you!"

says the gentleman, and he climbs the stairs. A bearded man hops off and retrieves his bicycle from the rack in front.

Inside, eleven other people are sitting quietly like they would in any other bus, in any other city. For the most part they're students with earphones, looking slightly bored. Both the older gentleman and the shy-looking lady sit down near the front, one behind the other. In the back of the bus an enthusiastic young man in a suit, shouldering a massive backpack, asks people around him what they're doing here today. Whatever they're willing to say, he generally finds it "awesome." Then he starts talking about himself, to no one in particular, or to everybody. He's an entrepreneur, he says. He's camping everywhere in the city, and so far he's started four companies. Ignoring the enthusiastic rambling, a group of students starts chatting loudly.

When it's almost time for the young entrepreneur and his massive backpack to leave the bus, he hauls it decidedly to the front and strikes up a conversation with Gaylene, the convivial bus driver. Gaylene is working three different routes this week: the 30, the 50, and also the 150. "Which one is your favorite?" someone asks. But she loves them all, especially because in each one of them, she says, she can see people of very different backgrounds and social classes. And all of them are just 'nice.' "People are people!" she declares, looking almost tenderly at her remaining passengers in the mirror before pulling the bus to a stop and wishing the young man a good one. He smiles, then promptly steps free of this strange pocket of banality and sets off to find his way again, back through the waiting sea of foreign luxury cars.

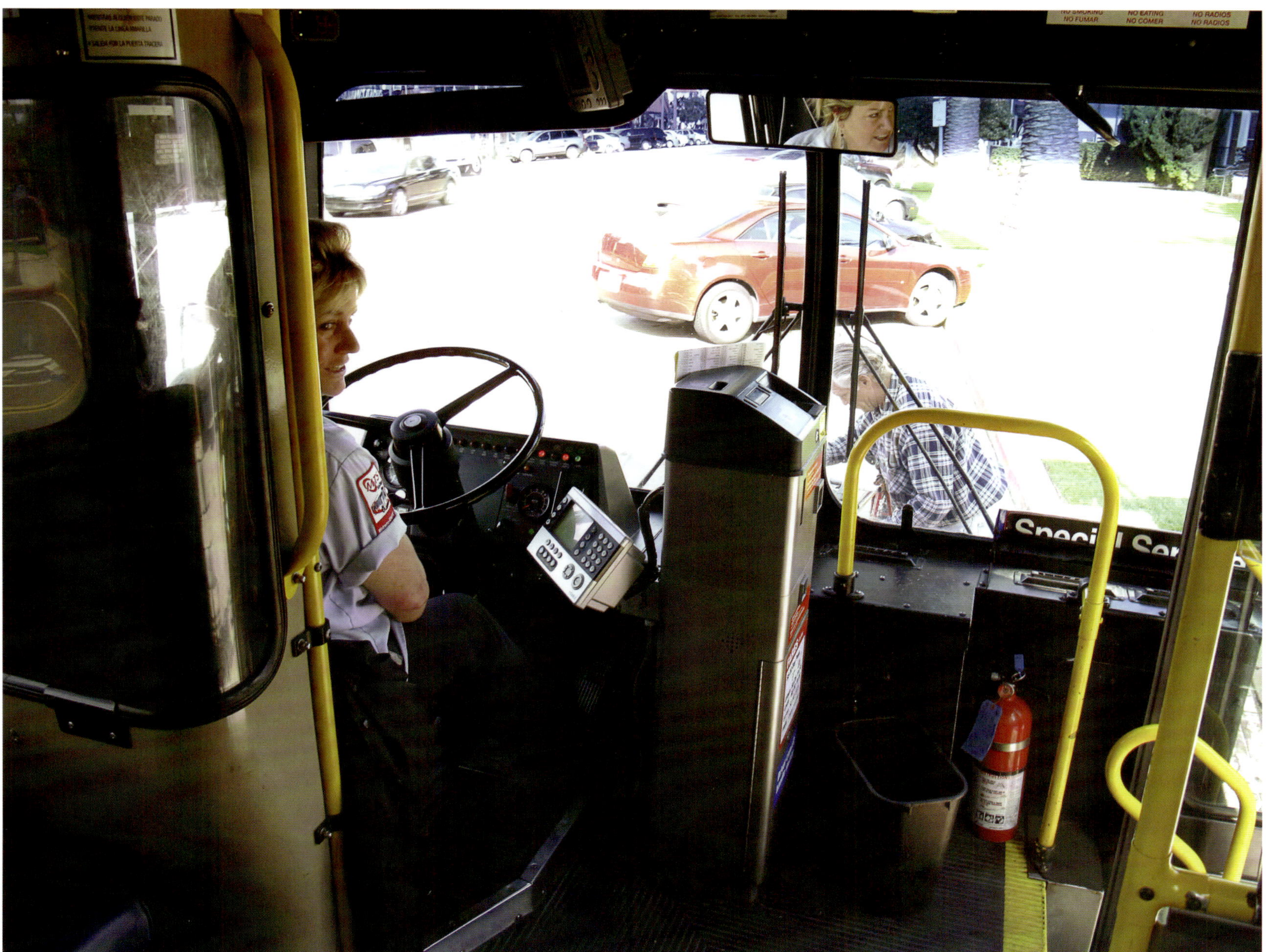

NO SMOKING
NO FUMAR
NO EATING
NO COMER
NO RADIOS
NO RADIOS
Special Service

When they arrive on top of Mount Soledad, people breathe a sigh of relief: the air is so light and deep, rich and inspiring. Lonely men and women crawl out of their cars; some of them have been driving all day. They take a few steps around an ordinary looking, 29-foot high white Latin cross made of concrete, then sit on a bench overlooking the wide spread of the city below and begin to think about all sorts of things. Rumor has it that this concrete cross was recently the object of a huge controversy, but standing here, closer to clouds than earth, it seems hard to believe.

Next to their red fire truck, a few firemen in yellow protective gear are spraying water on the dry bushes circling the mountaintop, probably as part of a training operation against future wild fires. One of them, an older man standing closest to the hydrant, smiles and waves at the lonely drivers ready for a meditative break. Everything looks so pretty, so perfect – almost artificially so. In the distance you can hear the last songs of the local birds and also, sometimes, the long siren of a train running up north along the Pacific coast on its way to Los Angeles. The unremarkable white cross pays them no mind, as heedless of its visitors as it is of supreme courts, former presidents, and the debates about its presence. Likewise unaware of any sound anywhere, a couple of sweating cyclists in Tour de France gear reaches the top on time. All they want in the world is some rest, some water, and an available bench overlooking the endless flow of minuscule automobiles moving up and down the freeway like numbers on a computer screen.

The one bench in front of them, however, which also has the best panoramic view of the sprawling neighborhoods and the brown condominiums fanned out at the foot of the mountain, is not going to become available any time soon. A couple of young hipsters in tight jeans and hats have appropriated it, and they seem to have no intention of surrendering their piece of stone. Maybe they've just escaped from school: they appear to be drunk with forbidden freedom as they kiss endlessly and joke about past events or funny characters in front of the whole city. "I love you!" screams the girl in a fake Italian accent; they kiss again and their laughter bubbles up anew. Behind them, the male half of an Asian family climbs its way toward the cross. The father keeps his professional-looking digital camera glued to his eye while the grandpa reads stories of fallen soldiers from past wars to himself, and two kids race their way up the stairs to the silent cross. There is no clear winner; it's all in good fun.

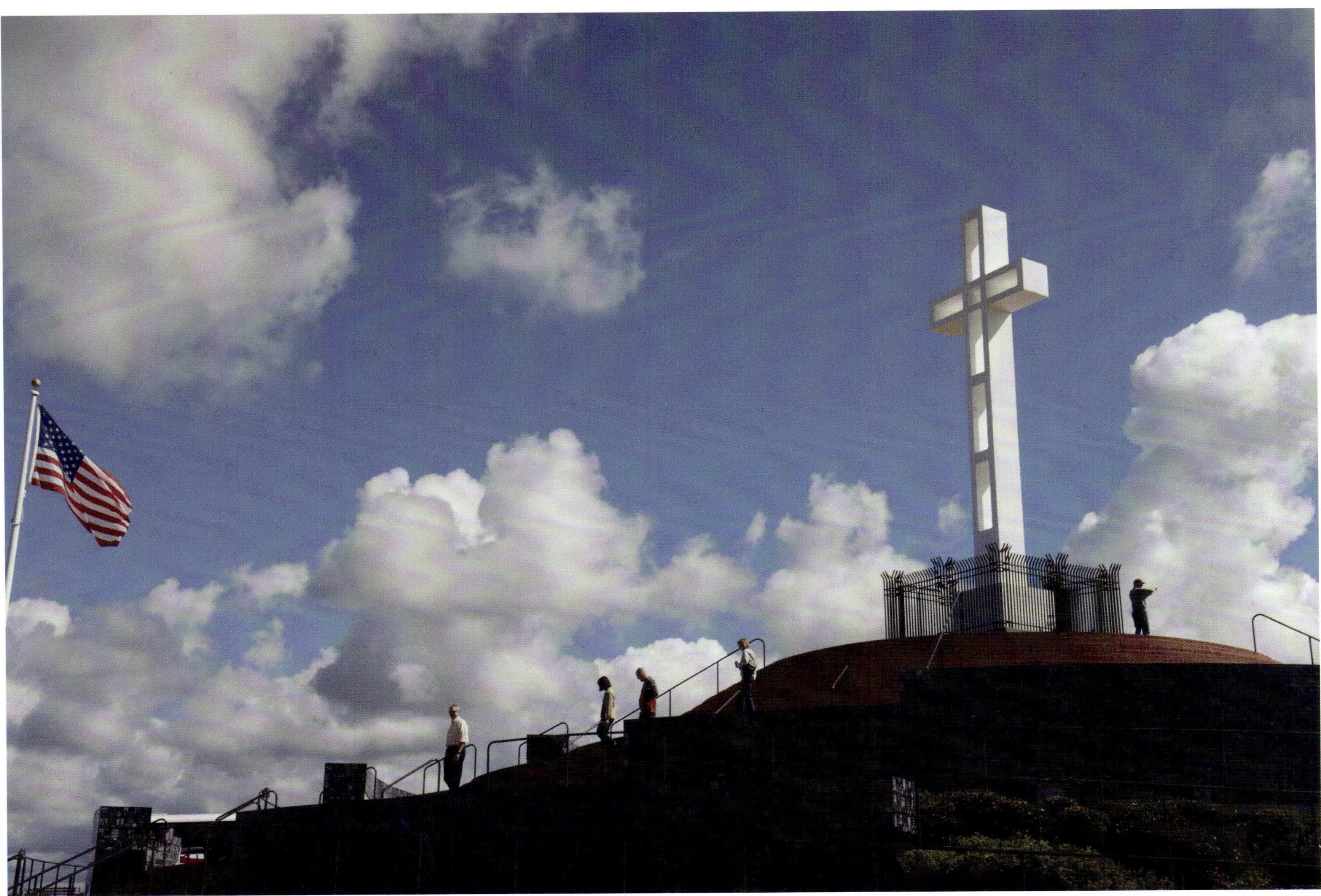

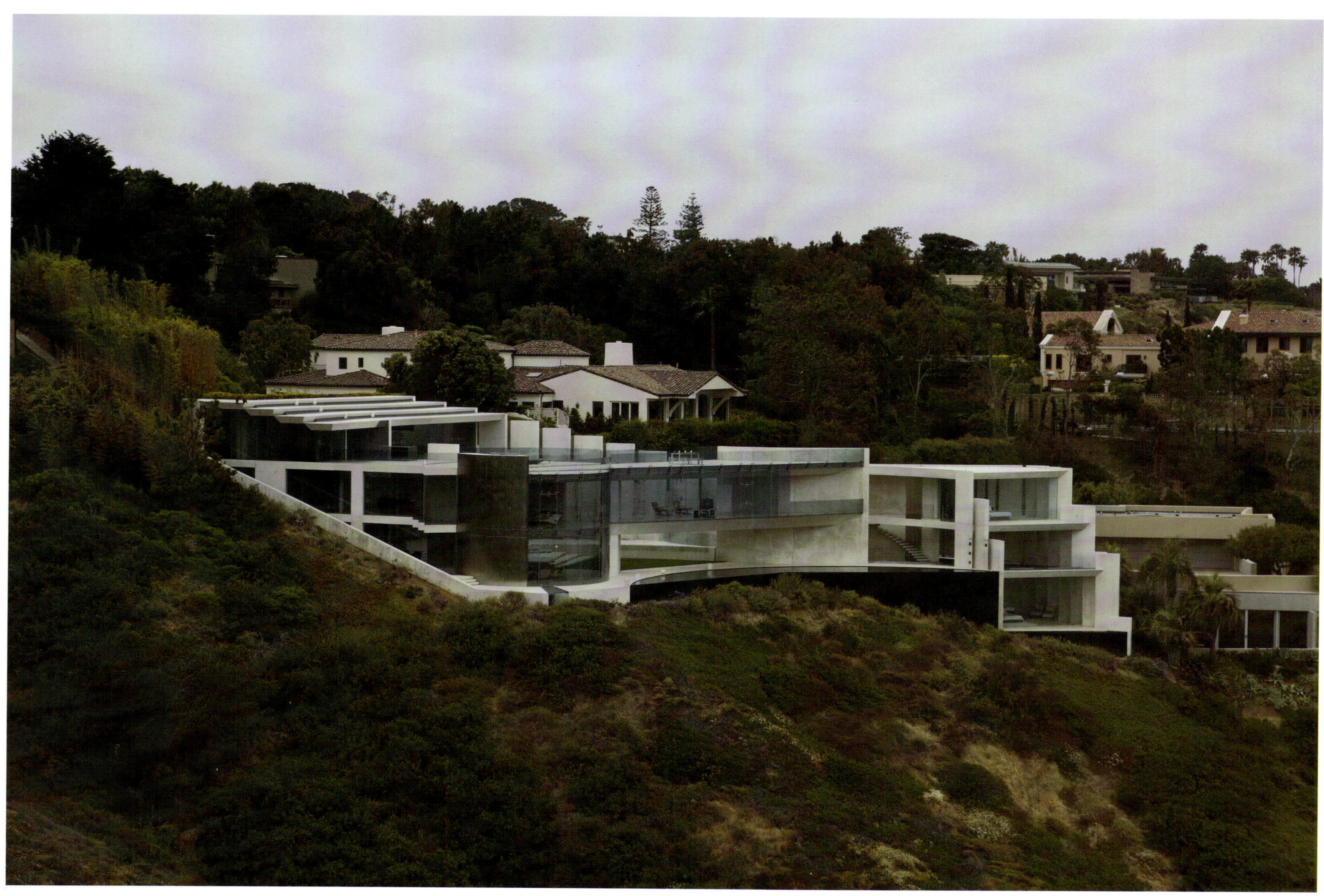

The Razor House, by architect Wallace Cunningham,
on the hills overlooking Black's Beach.

Hidden somewhere in the heart of the UC San Diego campus, at the head of a canyon, sits a strange building of concrete and glass surrounded by groves of eucalyptus trees. It is shaped to resemble a sort of giant, elaborate lantern reminiscent of an old tale from *One Thousand and One Nights*, albeit revisited by a futuristic mind. At the moment, two young Asian men, tall and skinny, are emerging from its base on skateboards, lazily rolling down the gentle slope. Their bodies are marked with discreet tattoos, their bags and T-shirts covered in apolitical emblems and signs: peace, rock musicians and brand names. In the grove across the way, tiny, lonely humans walk among the tall trees, lost in cell phone conversations.

Coming from the bottom of the canyon and approaching slowly, you might easily feel as though this puzzlingly modern structure is sprouting from the earth like an oddly shaped mushroom, its window-wall's changing color according to the sky's mood – an inviting hallucination. Another student on wheels, bigger and graver than his predecessors, is skating up toward the weird edifice, breathing hard as he tries to scale the canyon, like a furious bull. Small groups of young men and women trade jokes about finals and parties, then disappear into one of the forest houses nested in the adjoining enchanted clearing.

Along the narrow path winding around the lantern-shaped edifice, secretive young creatures, their features obscured by khaki green or black hoods, sprout from among the eucalyptus trees and cross back and forth between the forest houses. But despite appearances, they're not goblins or djinns; they're UCSD students. 99% of them ranked in the top 10% of their former high school, with a mean weighted GPA of 4.09 and an average ACT Composite Score of **28**. They circle the reflective mushroom, in truth a library designed by William Pereira, the "futurist" architect of Portuguese origins who later in his career also created the Trans-America pyramid in San Francisco and the Theme Building at the Los Angeles Airport. Some of the goblin-students disappear into their self-dubbed spaceship and scatter among its eight floors, looking to study or find a rare book. A sculpture of Dr. Seuss, for whom the library is named, watches them from his desk along with his most famous character, the Cat in the Hat. They are at home here, standing stoically in the shadow of this extraordinary building and its eerie surroundings, guarding a portal to other-worldly lands.

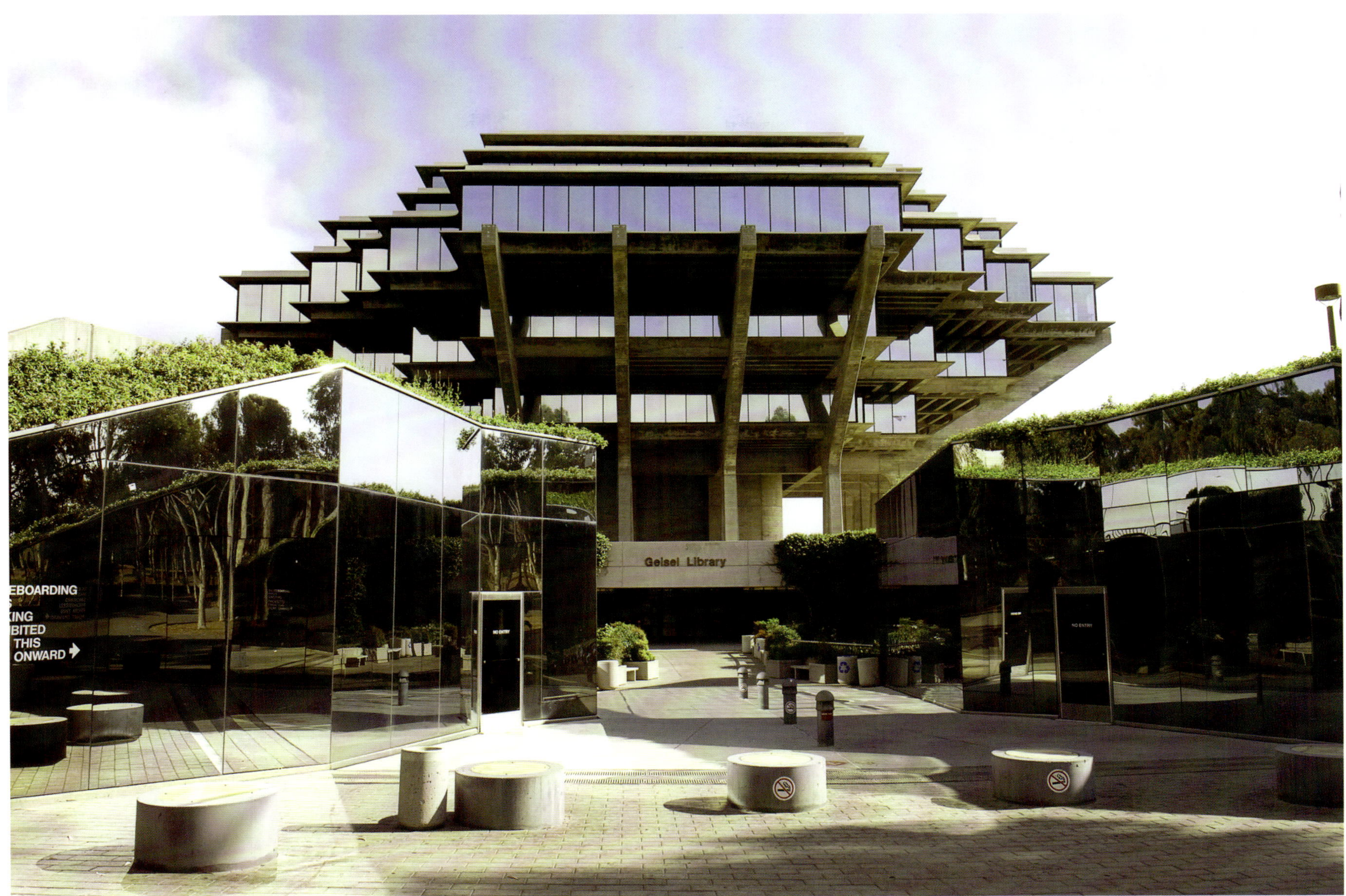
Geisel Library
EBOARDING
KING
IBITED
THIS
ONWARD
NO ENTRY
NO ENTRY

These days by the Cove, when the grass is still green and the ocean no threat, when the clouds are just fog drifting off into space, it feels like a truly mysterious place, and you can see the tree: the Dr. Seuss tree! The tree with the big fluffy top like a dream that all other trees strive to soothe and appease in the fresh morning breeze.

Not that long ago, not too far from the park, Dr. Seuss himself lived up on the hill. The rhythmical Doctor used to love to come down by the Cove for a stroll, seeking inspiration, and the phantasmagoric tree that was named after him is said to have been the model for some of his illustrations. He created, among so many fantastic characters, the Lorax: the *shortish, and oldish, and brownish, and mossy* creature that speaks for the trees.

I am the Lorax. I speak for the trees.
I speak for the trees, for the trees have no tongues.

At the age of 20, Theodor Seuss Geisel went to Oxford to become a doctor in literature, as his father wished. Instead, he met his future wife, Helen Palmer. He married her in 1927 and never became an official doctor in literature. Instead, he became Dr. Seuss.

His first book, *And to Think That I Saw It on Mullberry Street*, was inspired by the rhythm of a ship's engines on an ocean voyage he made in 1937. The book was turned down by 27 publishers, and young Theodor almost burned it. Today, there have been more than half a billion copies of Dr Seuss' 44 children's books sold.

He moved to La Jolla in 1946 and bought an old observation tower, in which he would shut himself away in a studio for at least 8 hours a day. He concentrated on his original passion, children's books, and remarried in 1968 to Audrey Stone Diamond after the death of his first wife, Helen. To this day, Audrey lives in their beautiful house on the hill, not far at all from the mysterious and fluffy tree that was named after him, down by the Cove...

Way back in the days when the grass was still green
and the pond was still wet
and the clouds were still clean
and the song of the Swomee-Swans rang out in space...
one morning, I came to this glorious place.
And I first saw the trees!
The Truffula Trees!
The bright-colored tufts of the Truffula Trees!
Mile after mile in the fresh morning breeze.

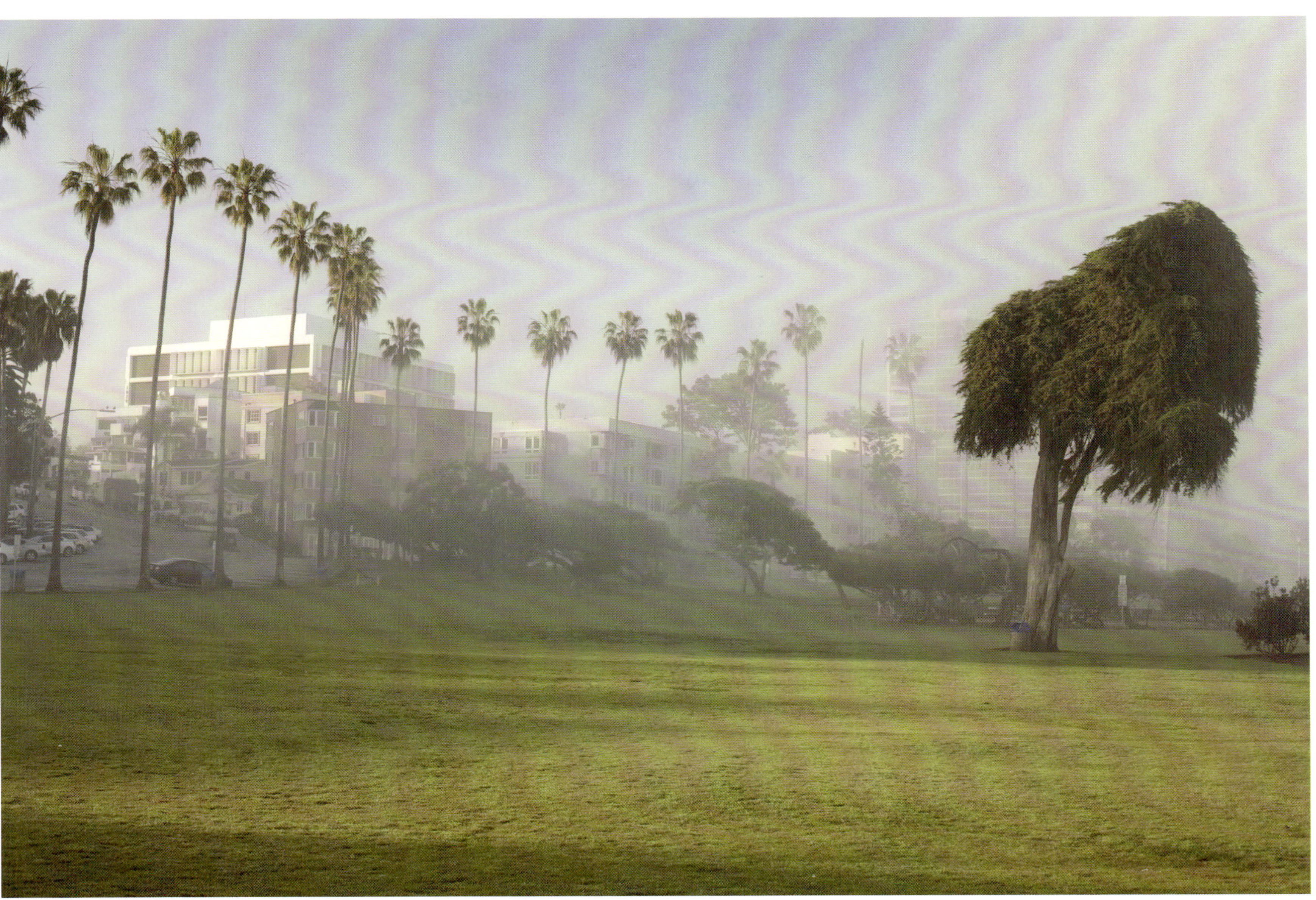

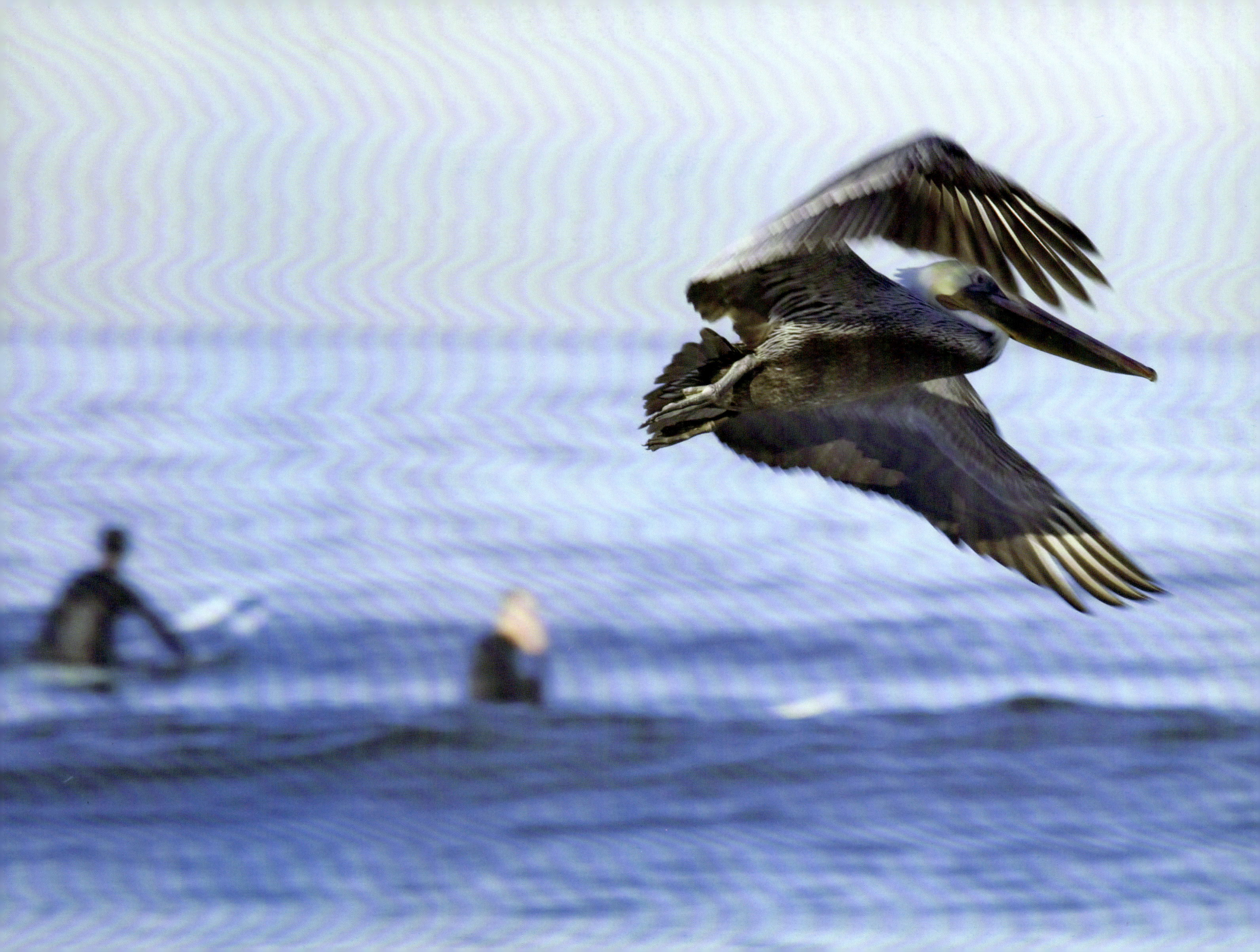

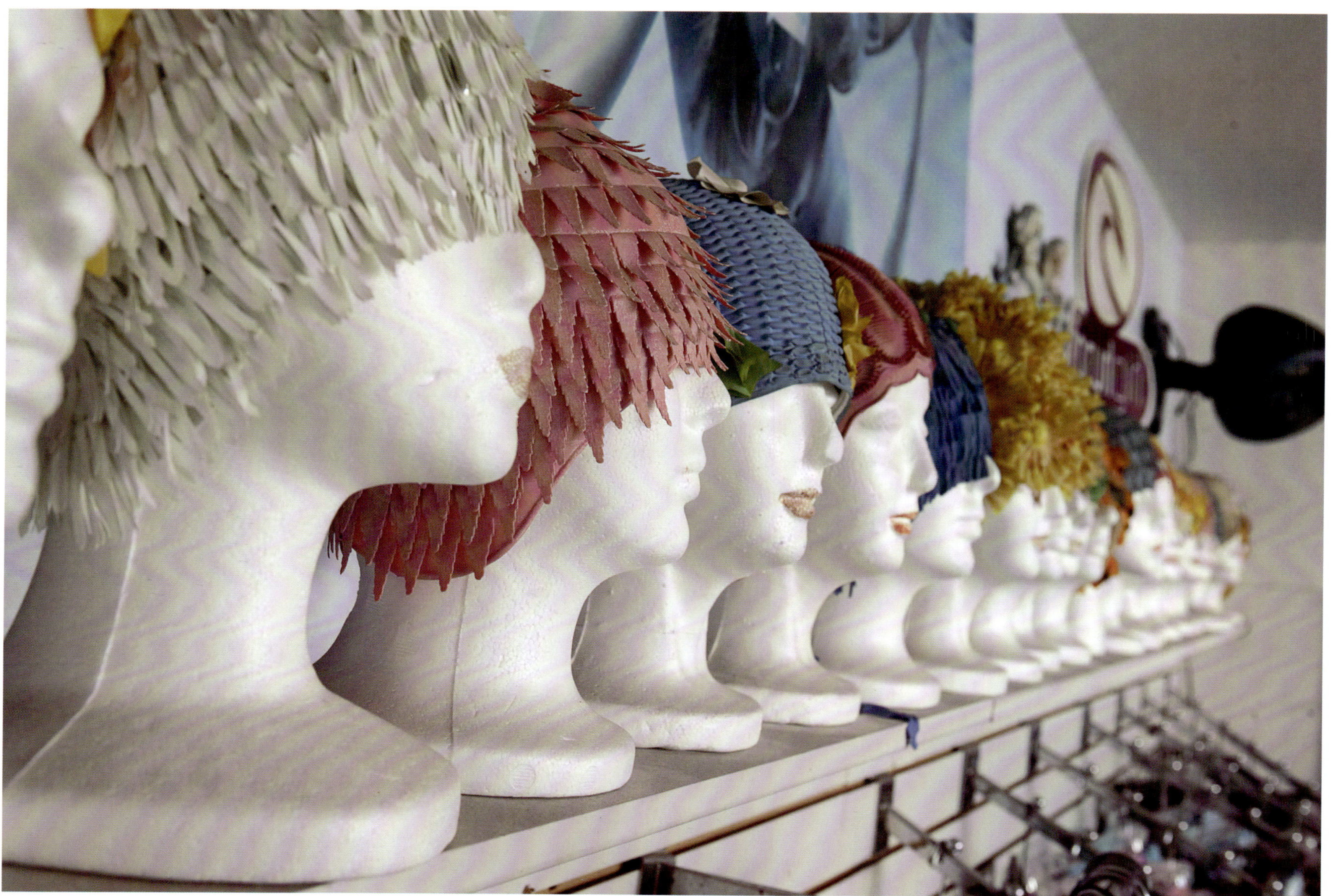

Highway 52 draws a straight line from the Arizona desert towns and mountains of the east to the beach community of La Jolla Shores. The end of the highway releases vacationers into a maze of charming residential streets. New arrivals might wander past the eccentric "Purple House," home to Dr. Klatt's mother, a woman known simply in the neighborhood as "the Purple Lady." A couple of blocks further down, the heart of Shores blossoms before their eyes, brimming with reckless cries and the smell of sunscreen. Some decide to hunt down a copious brunch at one of several eateries before venturing out onto the sandy beach. Others walk first, then dine out "farniente"-style at one of the two charming Italian restaurants facing each other on Avenida de la Playa. All around, customers slip in and out of small boutiques like the Ocean Girl store, clutching their newly purchased articles of beach and surf attire.

It is summer, and the streets around La Jolla Shores beach are almost as crowded as the sand itself. Surfers – looking decidedly like tribal warriors with white marks smeared on their foreheads – walk toward the beach or away from it as if in a daydream, weaving around families whose sunburn-reddened skin betrays their eastern or northern origins. The surfers stop at the corner of Avenida de la Playa and other more discreet residential streets to undress, uncaring of the ecstatic vacationers running small errands and soaking in the crisp, maritime air. A little group of foreign exchange girls aimlessly enters the Ocean Girl store on their way to the beach. If she has the time, owner and children's book author Terry Kraszewski might decide to show them her most treasured secret, in the back of her shop.

When she was younger, Terry was drawn to the statuesque images of elegant ladies wearing fashionable swim caps. Thus, 21 years ago, around the same time that she opened her first store, Terry started her own swim cap collection. It's now one of the coolest, albeit most discreet, attractions in La Jolla Shores. Most of her fascinating, stylish swim caps come from the 50's or 60's, an already long-gone era in fast-paced California. Eager to arrive at the beach with the right accessories for the day, the young exchange students haven't noticed them yet. Terry rotates 35 to 40 of them, and today she has 26 on display. Although they're not for sale, stately ladies born in a different era sometimes come in and ask for their price. They're always disappointed when told that they cannot try them on.

Every day on La Jolla Boulevard, cars pass by a strange little house with a traditional, iron-made, massive door and wonder what's going on inside. If they were to pull over and ring the bell, Louis Zalesjak would open the door and usher them in to a feast of tempting smells, old style décor, and some very good food.

After a life spent working in some of the most prestigious hotels in the world, Louis, who grew up in Slovenia, was thinking about opening his own quiet little restaurant. His dream: to serve fine French cuisine in a beautiful part of the world. The first step was choosing a location. He didn't like flat cities, and before long he had narrowed his choice down to four hilly places close to the sea: Monte Carlo, Rio de Janeiro, Vancouver, and La Jolla. That was **25** years ago.

Today, Louis is still pleased with his choice. La Jolla, he says, has the Mediterranean feel of Monte Carlo combined with the energy of the Pacific Ocean and the tranquillity of a small town. He opened his restaurant in Bird Rock, two blocks away from the sea, and for inspiration in choosing a name he turned to his personal history. Louis had kicked off his career as a demi-chef in Paris, training at the restaurants Maxim's, Tour d'Argent, and the Hotel Georges V for five years. From there he became a traditional "maître d'hôtel" and worked at ten successive hotels around the globe, including the Plaza Hotel in New York, the Dusit Thani Hotel in Bangkok, and the Carlton Hotel in Johannesburg. Reflecting on this, the name for his new restaurant in La Jolla seemed an obvious choice: *Maître D'.*

Now 73, Louis Zalesjak still owns what remains one of the best kept secrets in San Diego: a mysterious, somewhat intimidating old-style restaurant with only 12 tables where most of the city's big names, as well as some from way beyond, have stopped by for dinner. The walls of Maître D' are covered in pictures of Louis posing with famous guests like the king of Thailand and the Shah of Iran. "People don't come here to eat, they come to dine," says Louis, estimating off the top of his head that 80 percent of his guests order either the Steak au poivre flambé or the Steak Diane flambé. No one else in San Diego, he states proudly, does side-table preparation of flambées the way he does.

On May 25th, 2008, Louis Zalesjak celebrated the 25th anniversary of his restaurant. Despite not having advertised for it, a crowd of fine guests came to toast his success. And there were another 70 people already scheduled to stop by on the following Saturday, expected to order almost as many flambées.

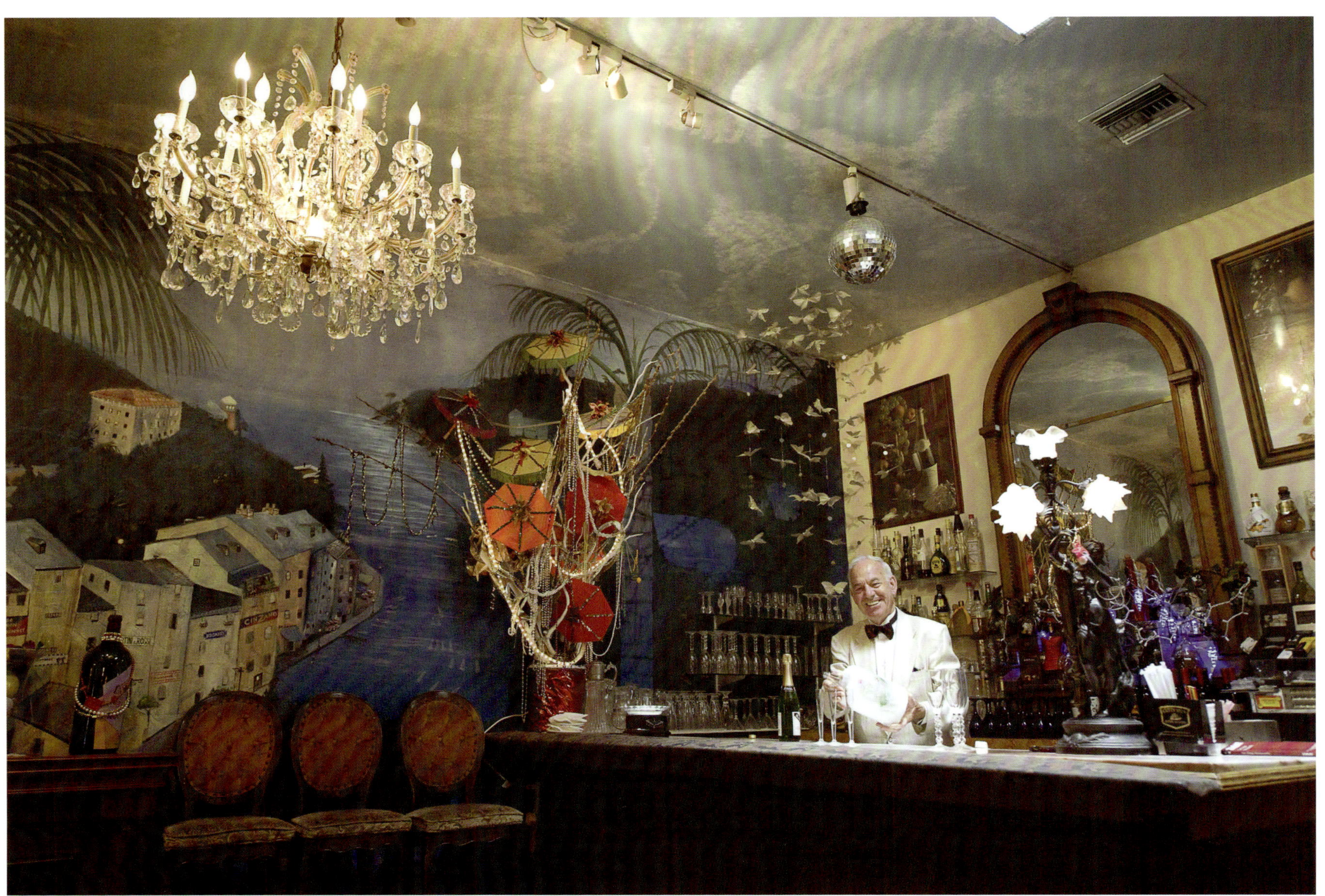

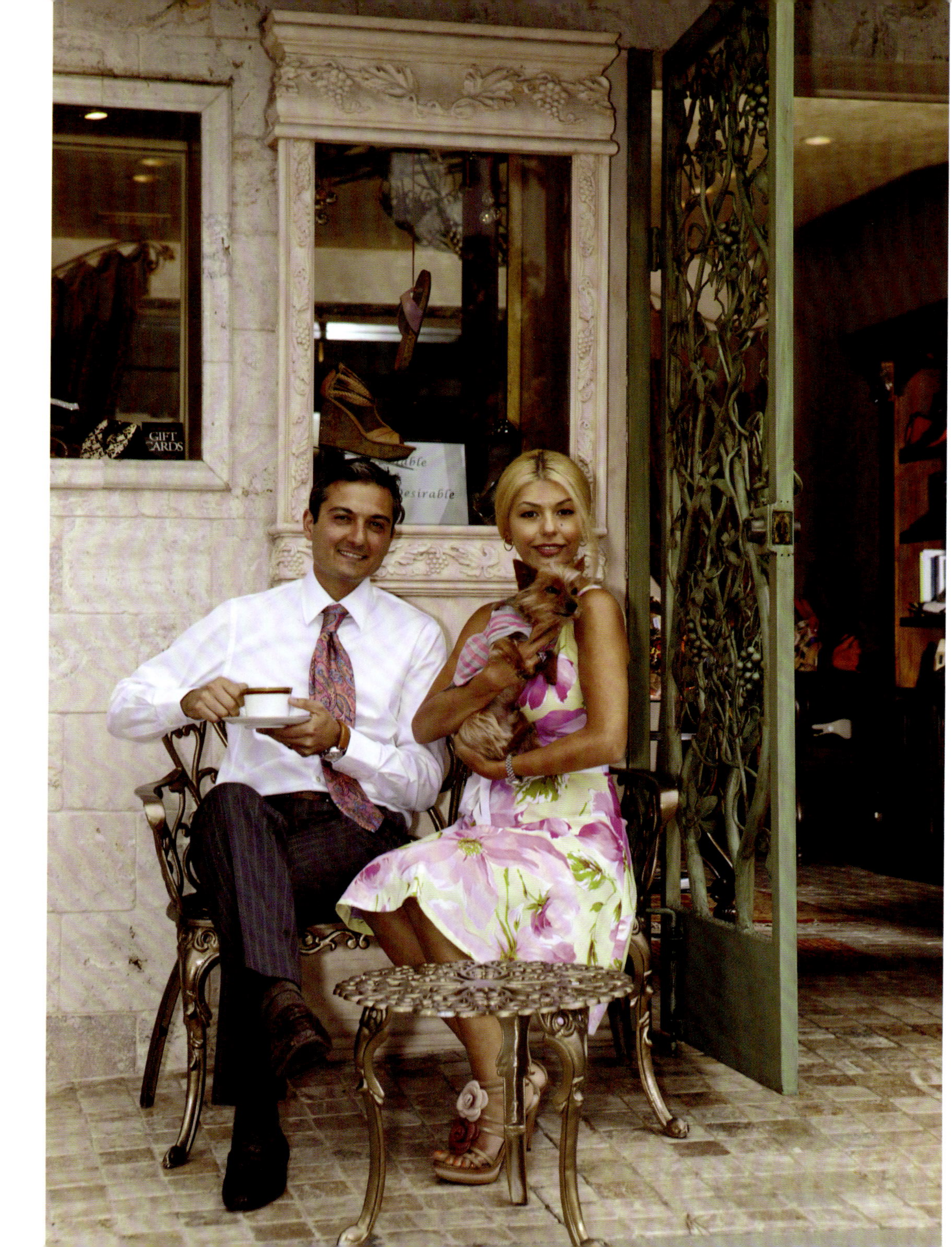

GIFT CARDS

Axel and Farnaz with their dog Maja
at the Serenity Shoe boutique.

Walking along the beach at Windansea when the colors of the late afternoon sky are at their most beautiful, one sometimes notices a fire engine cruising by with three strapping firefighters in the cab gazing at the reddish horizon through sunglasses. This is the crew from the Nautilus Street fire station, out on their occasional "sunset cruise."

At the Nautilus Street base, we meet and joke around with Captain Dan Guild and firefighter Michael Cates. "Firemen," Captain Guild says, "are like adults who have never grown up. They never got a real job!" However, everyone knows the dangers that firefighters constantly face in San Diego County, and most of what he has to say about La Jolla firefighters has more to do with work than play. The fire stations at Nautilus and on top of Mount Soledad, we discover, have one fire engine each at their disposal. At Shores, they've got one fire engine and an ambulance. On the other side of Highway

5, at the UCSD fire station, there's one fire truck. And the difference between a fire truck and a fire engine? "It's the ladder," reveals Captain Guild...

Of the 47 fire stations in San Diego, three lie within the 92037 zip code: the one on Nautilus, the one on top of Mount Soledad, and the one in Shores. In each fire station, three teams of four firemen work *24* hours shifts on blue, green, and red days, according to the fire department calendar. There is one female firefighter in the Nautilus Street station. She's been here for a while, and she's "very fit," according to the men.

So far this week, the Nautilus crew has received 22 calls. They always look ready to go, even when they talk to us and laugh. "Every kid dreams of becoming a firefighter or an astronaut," says Cates. "But you need to not take it too seriously,

and look at blood, fire and death with some distance." The Nautilus crew has heard somewhere that firefighters and nuns are supposed to be the happiest people in their jobs. As far as firefighters go, they can confirm this. And although they won't be prevailed upon to give us more details about the origin of their unusual hobby, we may see them later in the afternoon by the Pacific Ocean, when the sun starts its habitual descent to the horizon.

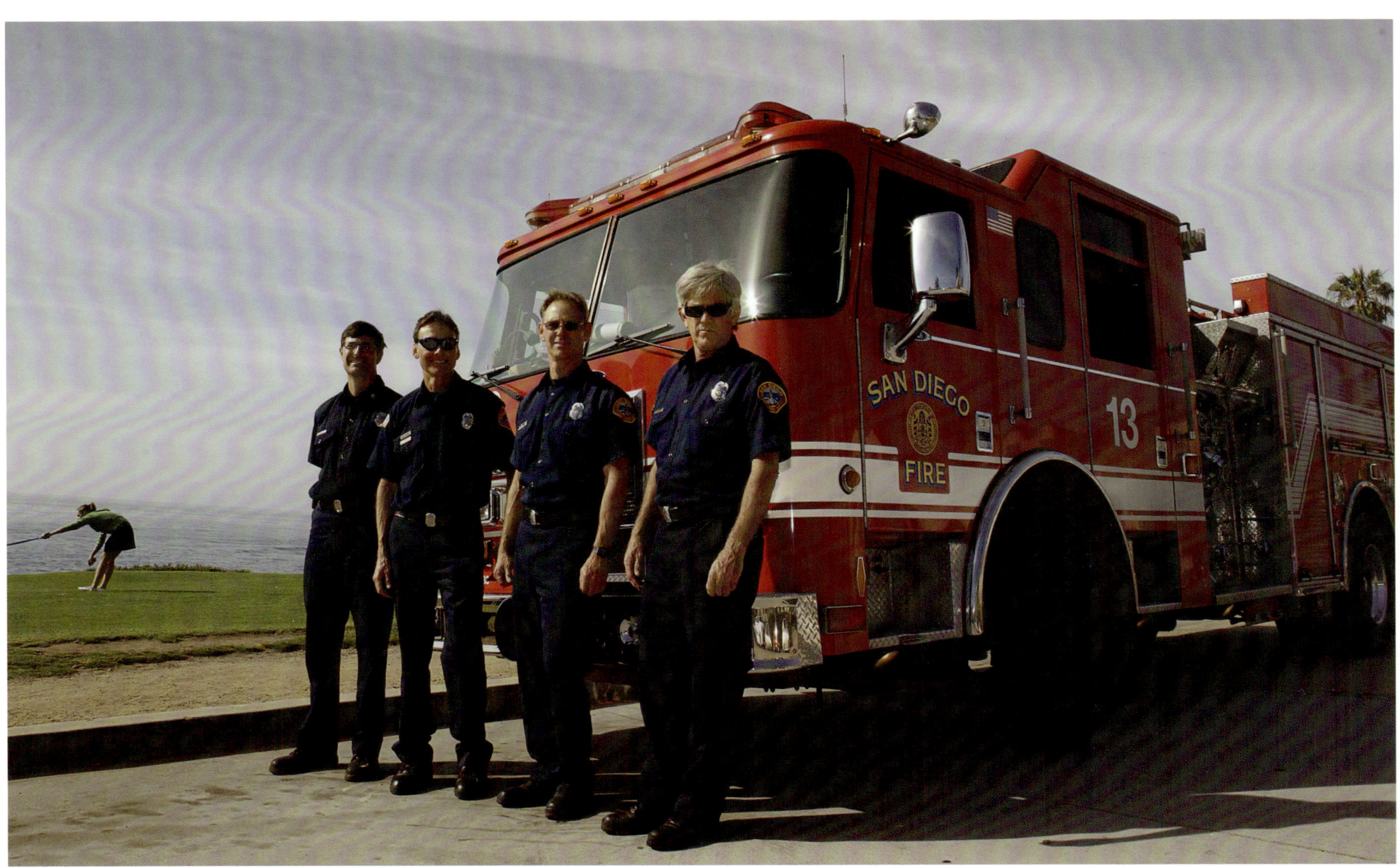

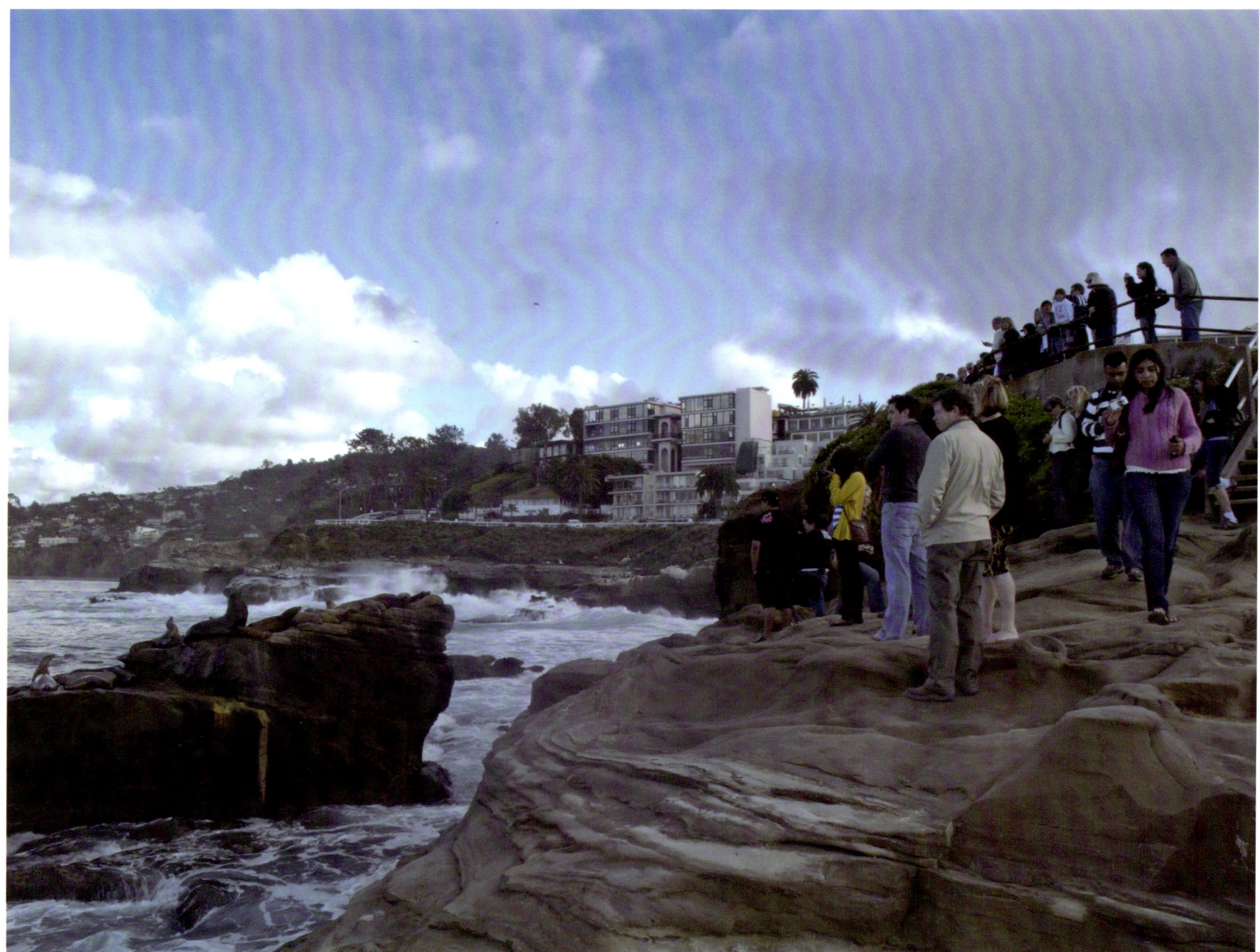

La Jolla is predominantly white. Recent counts turned up 35,166 Caucasians to 4,760 Asians, 2,992 Hispanics, and 359 African Americans. 3,223 foreign-born individuals arrived here in the 90's. At home, 72.9% of La Jollans speak English.

Among the 9,029 foreign-born residents, 51.3% of them are naturalized citizens. 12% are born in Mexico, 9% in Iran, 6% in Taiwan, and 6% in South Africa. 4,428 La Jollans are of English ancestry. 3,973 were originally Germans, 3,253 were Irish, 2,068 were Italians, 1,030 were Iranian, and 985 were French. Smaller groups include 333 people of Sub-Saharan African descent, 93 Israelis, 60 Iraqis, 12 Palestinians, 7 Maltese, and 6 Ethiopians. 5% each of the foreign-born population has roots in Germany, China, and Korea.

8.4% speak Spanish, 9.9% speak another Indo-European language, and 7.8% speak an Asian or Pacific Island language.

At the corner of Pearl Street and Cuvier, three Iranian stores next to one another create the closest La Jolla has to offer in terms of an ethnic neighborhood. Middle Eastern flavors and accents gather in this tiny part of town and meet with other accents from all over the world. The owners of the Sadaf restaurant, the Gabeh Rug Gallery, and the Sahel Bazaar & Deli in the alley next to it have all known each other for more than ten years, and together they attract a diverse crowd of local and international clients from Iran, India, and Europe.

The first people to start their business on this corner were Essy and Zari, who emigrated from Iran after the Islamic Revolution, first to Italy and then to California. They started the Sadaf restaurant in 1992 and have been serving their specialty lamb, chicken and beef kabobs, accompanied by delicious Basmati rice, ever since.

In 1999, Amjad and Sholeh became their next-door neighbors at the Gabeh Rug Gallery. They started out selling handmade antique rugs, 90% of them Persian. Nowadays, with about 1,000 rugs in their store, they do mostly repair and appraisal work for rugs that families have owned for generations. Sholeh reckons that an antique rug can last 200 years or more when it's properly taken care of.

In 2000, Amjad and Sholeh rented half of their space to Nasrin and Bijan, owners of the Sahel Bazaar & Deli. But when, some months ago, the rug sellers needed the extra room again, Sahel Bazaar moved to a charming, quiet location in a back alley, 50 yards or so away from the Rug Gallery. A table and two chairs in the shade of the patio provide a serene setting in which to taste some of the Bazaar's delicacies. With a staff of five, Sahel Bazaar offers its international and American customers everything from fresh fruits and veggies to all sorts of rice sold in twenty-pound sacks, including Jasmine Rice at $10, India Gate Rice at $15, and Kohinoor Rice at $23. It also sells hundreds of rare products such as imported Persian tea, Turkish coffee, couscous, rose water, fresh humus, Bulgarian feta, Greek Kalamata olives, hard-to-find Fig preserves, pomegranate juice, spicy chutney, grapeseed oil, and even some ready-made dishes like Tabouleh and Greek salad.

Even half an hour spent in this rare sample of exoticism in La Jolla is enough to expose you to the Russian, German, French, and Middle-Eastern accents of customers stopping by, often mixed with the rhythms of Persian music (also for sale). Outside on the patio, a young couple from Europe eats a Greek salad and grape leaves put together by Nasrin, the owner, who serves them tea with a generous smile while greeting a large Indian family at the door of the Bazaar. By the looks on their faces, Nasrin will be serving quite a few more grape leaves before the day is out.

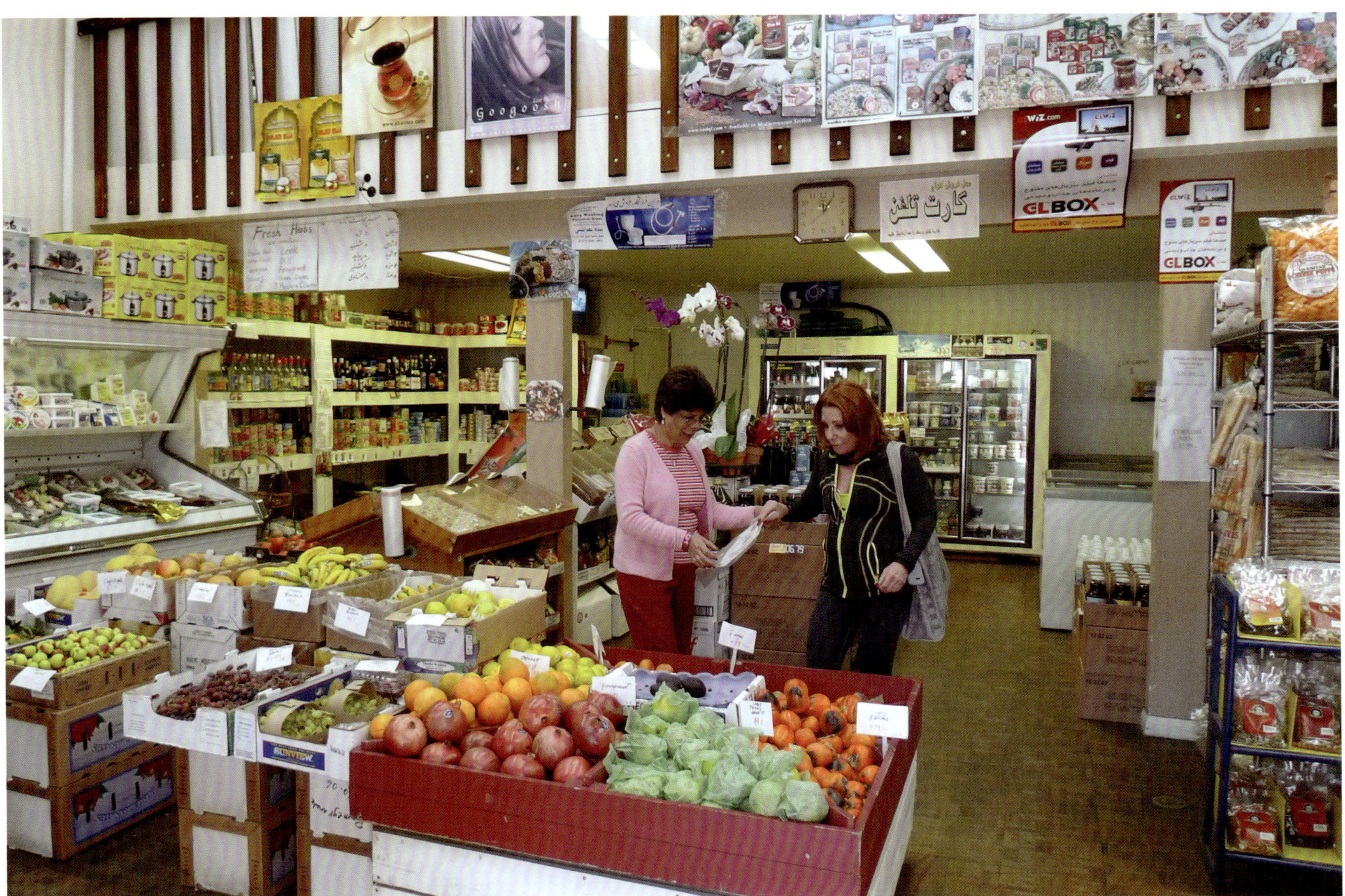
Fresh Herbs
Leek
GL BOX
GL BOX
Googoosh

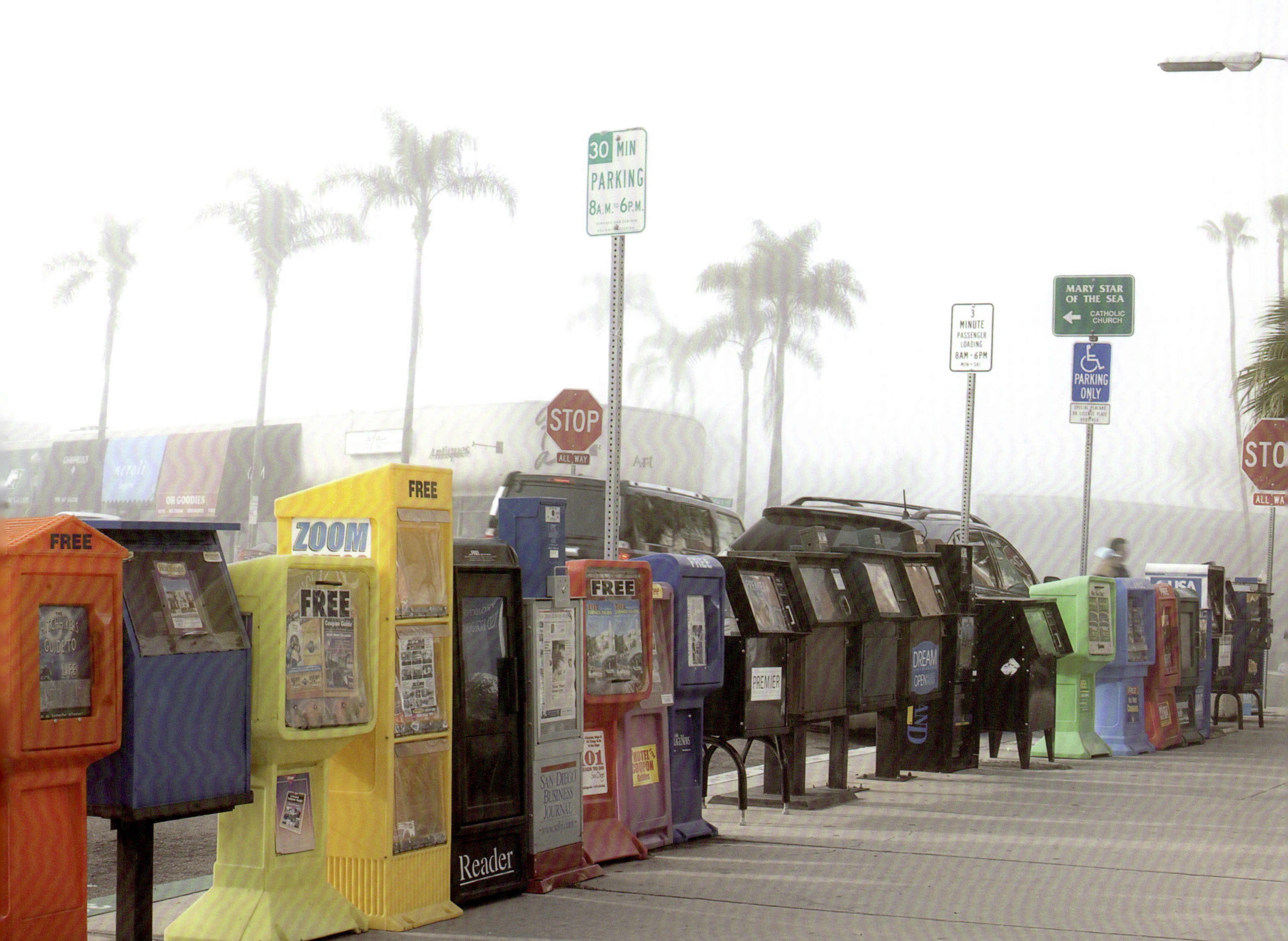

30 MIN
PARKING
8 A.M. TO 6 P.M.
STOP
ALL WAY
3
MINUTE
PASSENGER
LOADING
8AM-6PM
MON-SAT
MARY STAR
OF THE SEA
CATHOLIC
CHURCH
PARKING
ONLY
STO
ALL WA
FREE
FREE
ZOOM
FREE
FREE
FREE
Reader
San Diego
Business
Journal
www.sdbj.com
PREMIER
DREAM
OPEN
HOTEL
COUPON
101
Antiques
OH GOODIES

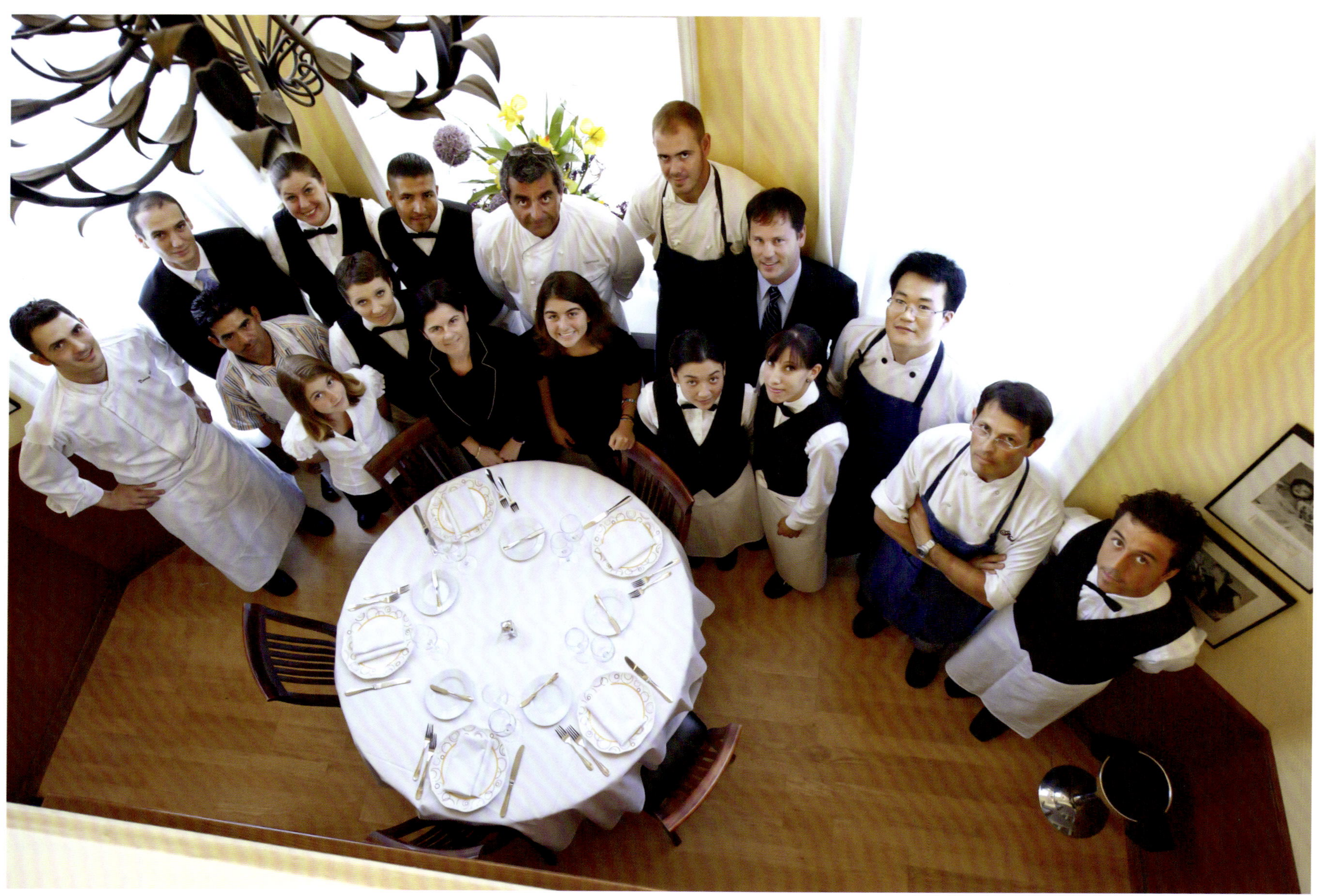

The little corner of La Jolla where Tapenade is located presents the usual scene of a typical wealthy, coastal community. There are quaint mini-malls with clothes boutiques and pastry shops, restaurants with wide, closed patios, couples of customers in chic business-casual attire, and a large supermarket parking lot filled with brand new, shiny cars. But inside the warmly-lit restaurant that looks like an intimate Parisian bistro, Jean-Michel and Sylvie Diot, the French owners of Tapenade, remember that it wasn't always this way.

In the early nineties, they were living in New York, in an apartment facing the Empire State Building, when they decided to visit San Diego to see the America Cup. One evening, following their sightseer's whim, they wandered into La Jolla. Nature was in full bloom and everything seemed so pretty, so peaceful and healthy. They found they couldn't leave, and five years later they took their two young daughters and left Jean-Michel's four successful French restaurants and brasseries in Manhattan to start a new one by the Cove.

Despite their New York friends' skepticism that San Diegans wouldn't "get it," they found a venue on Fay Avenue in what was a very rundown neighborhood at the time, filled with empty old buildings and homeless drunks. Thus, Tapenade was born.

Today, sitting at one of Tapenade's tables draped in an immaculate white cloth, you are served by impeccably mannered, flawlessly dressed waiters captained by the classy and dry-humored Ludo. A couple of sips of perfect Chablis wine eases the intimidation of the classic elegance of it all, and you start to give your palate free reign, letting it revel in the cutely creative "amuse-bouches" and the dark, rich tapenade that is the restaurant's signature spread. You taste your first escargot and it's hot on your tongue, hitting you fast and then, slowly, deliciously, melting away into the corners of your mouth. Remembering to look up, you catch a glimpse of Chef Jean-Michel quietly touring the tables. When he arrives at yours, silent and shy with an astute expression in his eyes, you try to give him your full attention, but to no avail:

the buttery escargot sauce is too addictive, and you can't resist dipping into it again. Jean-Michel smiles, and nods approvingly.

With **22** employees at the start, Tapenade as a whole was an instant hit, and it largely contributed to the reformation of the neighborhood. It also initiated a culinary revolution of sorts in La Jolla. George's changed its chef, and other fine restaurants such as Nine/Ten and Roppongi opened a short while after, their universal success proving that La Jollans were ready for the gourmet experience. Niki de St Phalle was a regular at Tapenade until a few days before her death, when she was ordering its soups to her hospital room. But for those still in good health, it's so much more pleasant to dine on site, surrounded by black and white photos of Paris and old French movies. Hours of ageless flavors later, they leave this little French corner with smiles on their satisfied mouths and hands caressing their stomachs, returning unhurriedly to the transformed neighborhood of quaint mini-malls around them.

"California has been a rebirth for my soul and an earthquake for my eyes—sea, desert, mountains, wide open sky, brilliance of light and vastness of space," said Niki de Saint Phalle. She moved from Paris to La Jolla in the nineties, and fanciful reminders of her excursion through the area are spread out around the county for anybody to casually encounter, most often with surprise or delight.

One of them is standing somewhere in the sculpture garden of the museum of contemporary art, located just in front of the ocean. Despite the slightly foggy day, it isn't too difficult to find it among the other modern creations. Its vivid colors and weirdly childish shapes stand out in the calm setting, and on the weekends or during summer vacation there's often a little crowd of young kids playing around it.

Universally overjoyed at the mere sight of Niki's colorful work of art, the museum's smaller visitors have a hard time keeping their hands off of this 11-foot version of the elephant-like Hindu god of good fortune and wisdom. They hug it or make fun of its large belly; they laugh, they scream, and sometimes they even spray water at each other around it with the sculpture garden's yellow hoses.

Big Ganesh seems to enjoy the scene and no doubt Niki herself wouldn't have minded the loud and uncontrolled attention her sculpture receives. She was first noticed because of the interactive violence encouraged in her early exhibitions in Paris. Her "Target" paintings invited viewers to throw darts at them, while her "Shooting" paintings were shot at with paint, thus actually making them.

Niki de St. Phalle was living not far from here, in a contemporarily-designed house on a quiet street en route to La Jolla Shores. Even when she became gravely ill, people around her remember how she never ceased to be highly excited by anything new and beautiful. She died a few years ago on the 21st of May, in La Jolla.

The year after she passed away, *Queen Califia's Magical Circle Garden*, her last public work inspired by the early California legend of a black Amazon queen, opened in Escondido. There too, children climb up, over and through the sculpture pieces the same way they do with *Big Ganesh* in front of the foggy ocean. In the presence of these statues, they are unstoppable. Ignoring their tired parents' admonitions, they keep on playing with the wildly colorful elephant-god, running around it tirelessly and letting loose screams of laughter that seem to ricochet off the artwork, going on and on until late in the day.

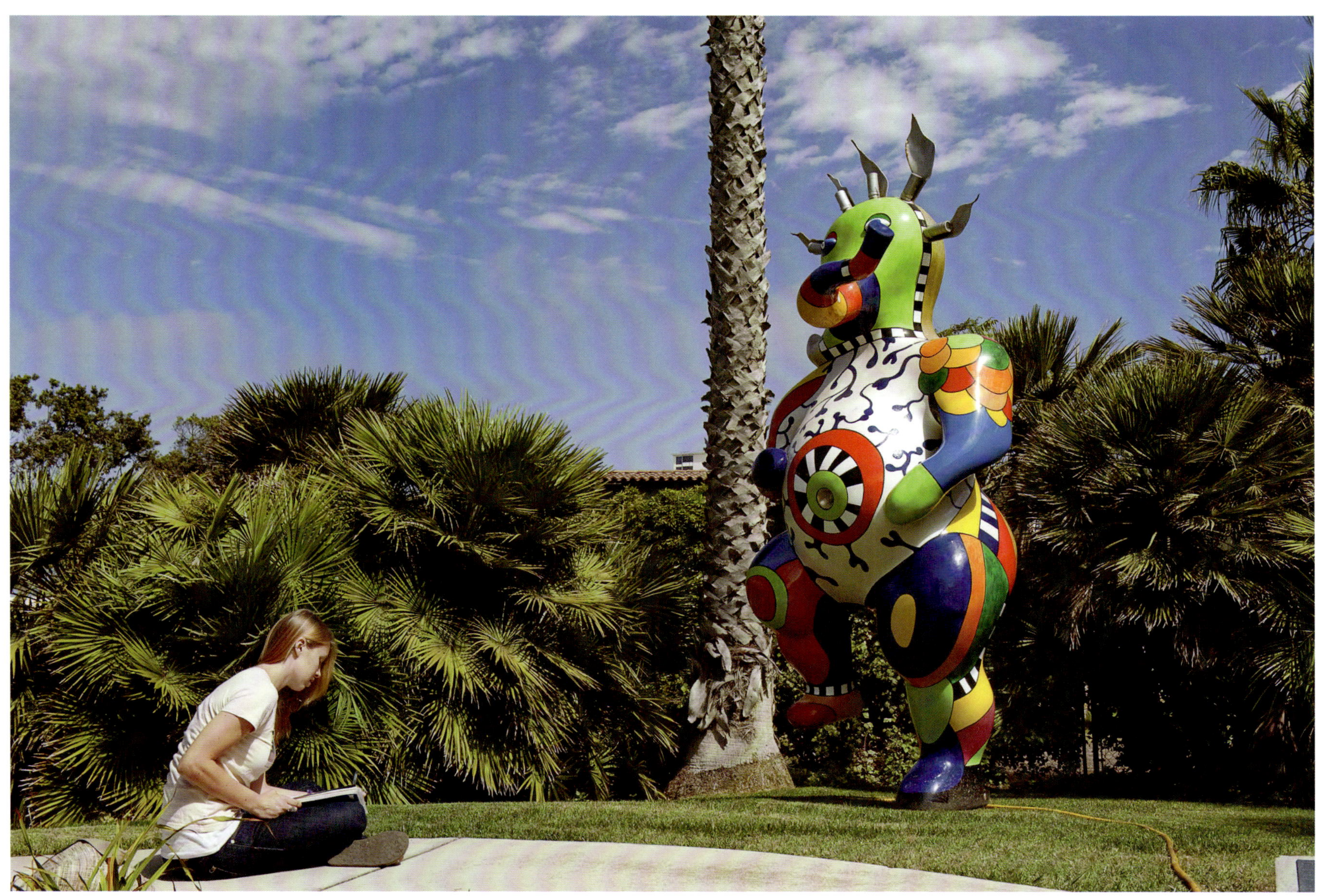

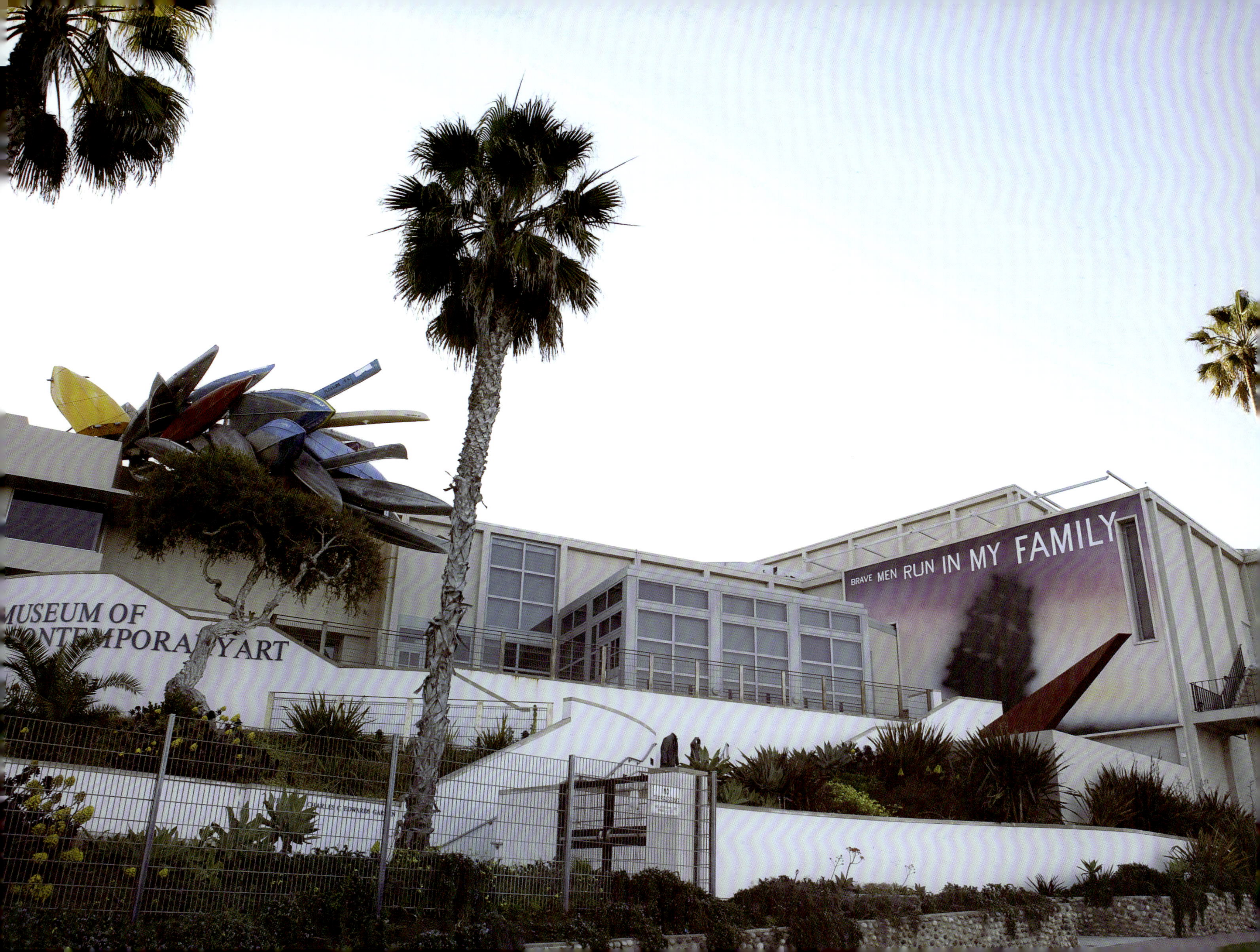

MUSEUM OF
CONTEMPORARY ART
BRAVE MEN RUN IN MY FAMILY

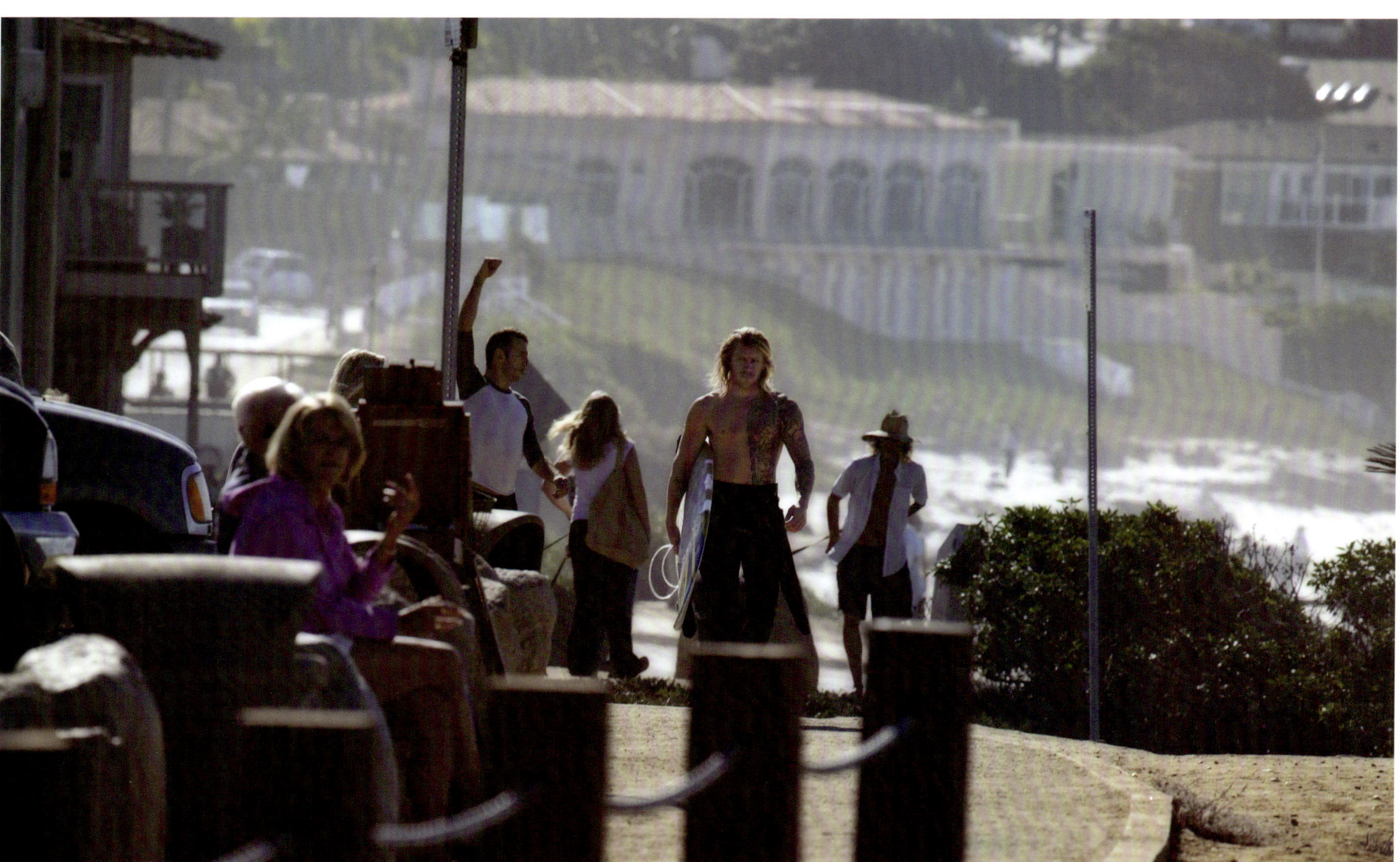

"La Jolla has something to be really proud of at Windansea," said storyteller and surfing pioneer John Elwell. "It has some of the best breaks in the world."

Windansea Beach is indeed one of the most important surfing spots in California, one that still fascinates – and intimidates – novice surfers from everywhere around. The 60's especially, considered by many to be the golden age of surf, saw the biggest names in the sport take on Windansea's reef break, names like Bob Simmons, Butch Van Artsdalen or Mickey Munoz. Looking out on the ocean, it doesn't take long to figure out why they've become legends: the waves here are perfectly shaped towers that, according to some, can soar up to *20* feet high.

A local guy with a black sweater and long, blond hair that's slowly turning gray is watching the few surfers struggling to catch their last wave before sunset on this windy day. This area was named after an oceanfront hotel that burned down in the 40's, but if he knows about it he doesn't really seem to care, lighting up another cigarette. These days, the main landmark at Windansea is a simple palm-covered shack, facing the classic reef break that has won the beach its reputation. Also constructed in the 40's by three eccentric locals to provide shade, a changing room and a locker for their boards, it soon became the center of the annual summer party called the *Luaus*, a gathering so out of control that the police were forced to put a stop to it in the 50's. It is this wild place that inspired *The Pump House Gang*, a Tom Wolfe novel published in 1968 that popularized the extreme life-style of local surfers.

As of 1998, the surf shack has actually become an official San Diego landmark, and in the summer surfers of positively all ages wander in and around their stronghold, happy to share it as well as the ocean waves with the bikini-clad swimmers. Now and then they stop to stare up at the private jets crisscrossing the sky overhead, or the occasional military helicopter training for the wars in the Middle-East. Firemen coast down here in their truck to check the scene in the late afternoon, sometimes crossing paths with drunk, party-seeking hipsters clad in stylish bathing suits. The revelers dance to electronic music, hip hop, or remixes of British pop hits from the 90's played by a friendly DJ, also in a bathing suit. However, nowadays they carefully turn off the music half an hour after sunset, before the police get any complaints. No riots in sight.

Everyone in La Jolla knows Dr. Klatt, or at the very least they've seen his proud silhouette walking in the village with one of his seeing-eye dogs. This morning he is out with Lawson, a beautiful, calm German shepherd. Lawson is the sixth seeing-eye dog Dr Klatt has had since his world went black at the age of *19* more than four decades ago.

Dr. Klatt has memories of La Jolla in the fifties, before his nineteenth birthday, when it was nothing more than a sleepy little fishing town. Back then, fishermen used to drive down his family's street to get to the boat dock in La Jolla Shores. When Dr. Klatt was nineteen, he was a happy student, a life guard and a surfer. Then the accident happened.

"I was driving a 1955 Oldsmobile," Dr. Klatt wrote, "when the left front tire blew out and the car careened over a cliff, crashing 150 feet below. My face hit the metal dashboard of the car. I broke my jaw and my nose, my facial bone structure shattered and my optic globes burst. My left leg was ripped open and was bleeding profusely. Spinal fluid was leaking through my nose. My rescuer found me several hours later. In the Emergency Room the doctors infused three pints of blood. The doctors did not expect me to live another 24 hours."

But Dr. Klatt did survive. The year was 1967. He finished his studies, majored in Speech, Philosophy and Psychology, and completed a special training program at the Seeing Eye school in New Jersey.

Today, Dr. Klatt is a successful realtor with an office next to the La Jolla post office, at 1124 Wall Street. He's been working at this address since 1978, managing his own business after six years working for a real estate agency located in the Arcade Building.

And now, every day of the week, La Jollans and tourists alike pause and take note of that proud silhouette, walking sedately with Lawson on its way to work in the heart of the village.

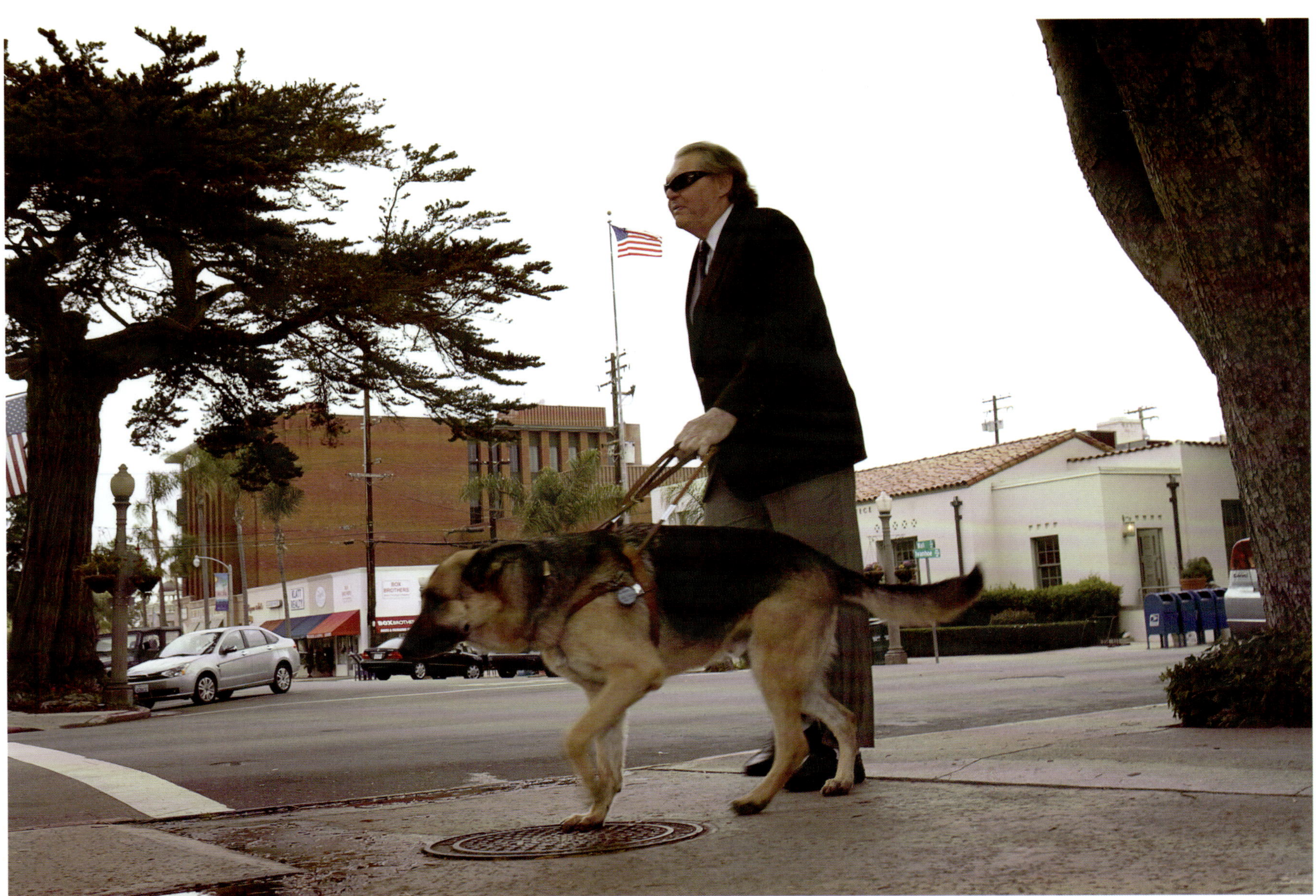

If you're looking for a sports car or a very high-end automobile, you came to the right place. There are no less than three sports and luxury car dealers in the "village" of La Jolla, one on Girard Avenue and two on La Jolla Boulevard, all within a few hundred yards of each other. And if you feel this urgent need for a sports car immediately, be it for a couple hours of flashy cruising or just a 30-minute emergency, you also came to the right place. *San Diego Prestige*, a company located in the same village and owned by French expats, rents Ferraris by the hour.

There are some days when you can't just show up in your regular BMW, like every other average Joe. Such incidents tend to happen in seasons, like when every other driver is a snobby New Englander on vacation in his multi-million-dollar second home. These interlopers hum along in their convertibles like they've never seen the sun or a palm tree set against a pure blue sky before. Their hair whips idly in the air behind them and they hum louder, as if determined to be *18* years old again – at least for the duration of the drive.

And then there are the cocktail parties, and the Golf Open. There are the yearly charity balls, the family reunions or the business dinners with prestigious guests from abroad. Yes, occasions are plenty when you need an extra-special jewel of a car in La Jolla, and the sooner you can start buying or even renting an out-of-the-ordinary vehicle, the better. A new Ferrari starts at $250,000 at *Sports Car Company*, whereas a new Rolls Royce's at *Symbolic* will set you back $370,000. As a temporary alternative, renting a Ferrari 360 at San Diego Prestige will cost you $995 per 24-hour cycle. Note that cheaper brands like Maserati or Bentley may very well produce similar effects.

Yet, where La Jolla Boulevard begins, when the night has fallen and the intimidating sales representatives are gone, the lights stay on and tiny groups of admirers come near the shop windows to look at cars they can't afford from every possible angle. Frequently they are silent, like the faithful of ancient Christian times gazing on idyllic depictions of the Calvary. Oblivious to the outside world, they linger for hours, licking their ice creams sprinkled with chocolate candy and dreaming of more expensive treasures.

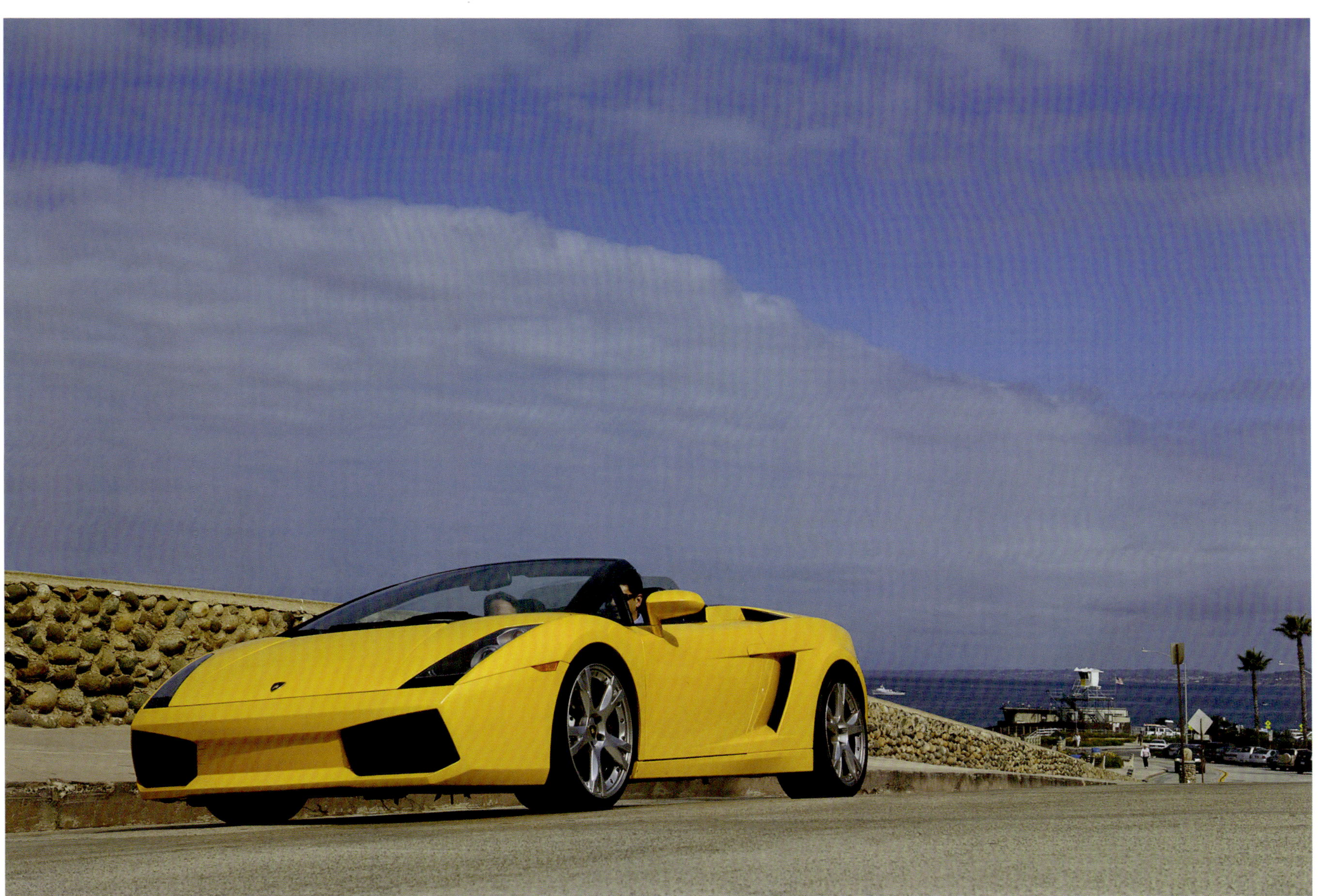

La Jolla-based architect James Alcorn in his 1939 MG VA,
which he brought back from England.

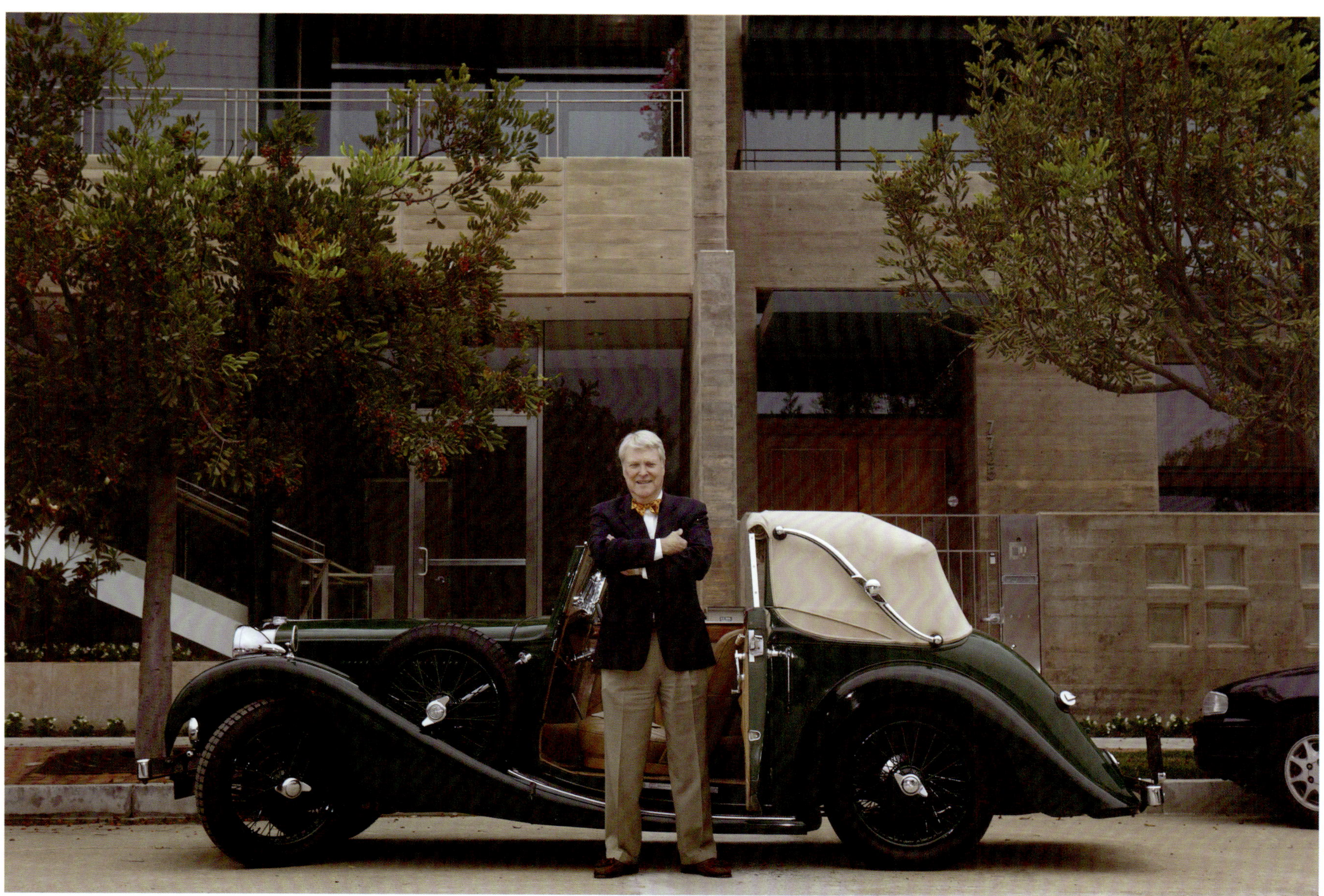

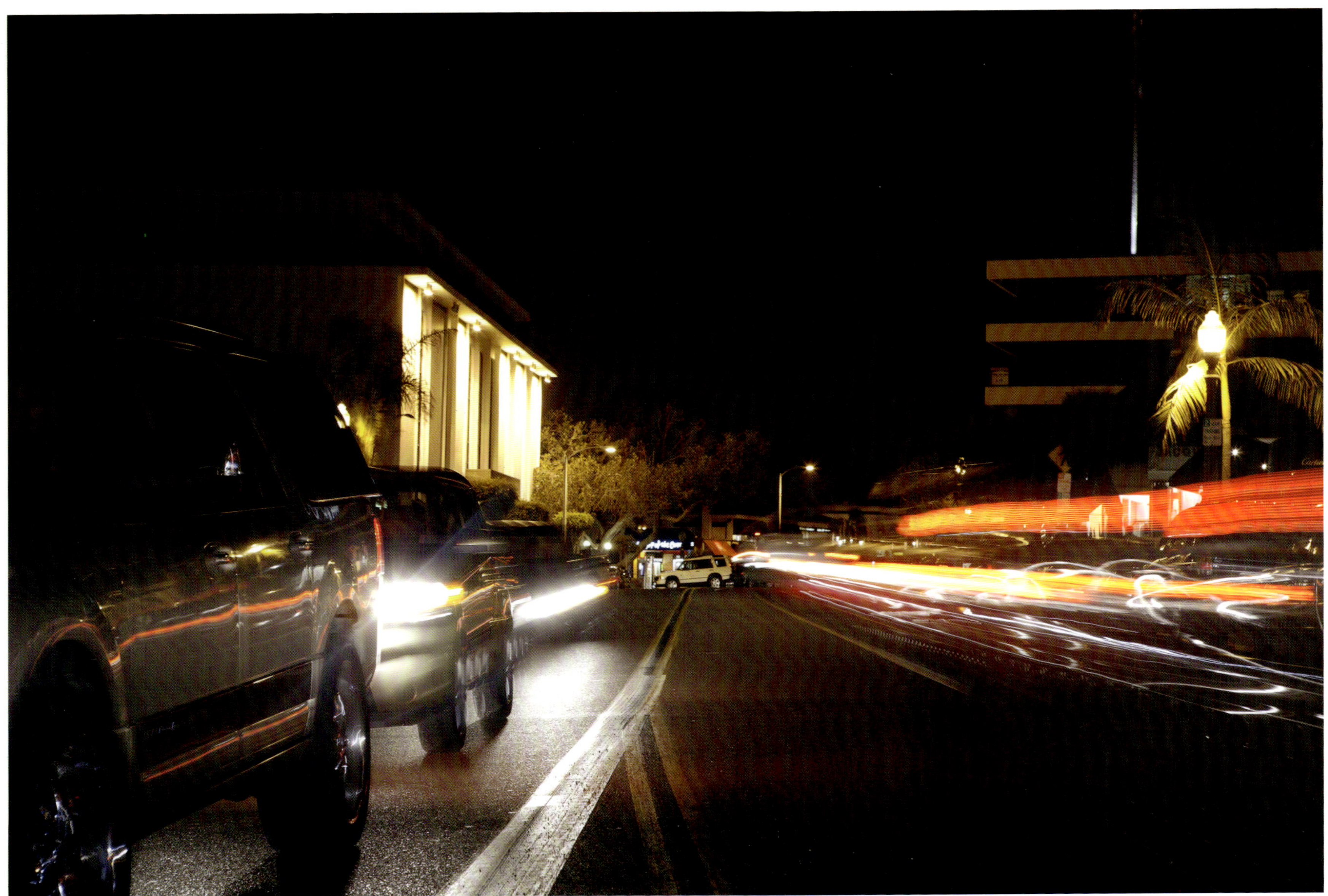

La
Jolla is one of the very few
areas in San Diego where people could live
quite comfortably without a car. However, only 2.2% –
or 940 people – in the zip code choose to do so. 17.5% of the population
owns two vehicles. 6,616 people own only one, and 182 people can boast at least 5 cars or trucks.
People who own their homes tend to own more vehicles than those who rent apartments. 70% of working La
Jollans drive a car to work. 9% walk, 6% carpool, and 3% ride a bike. Only 2%
of them use public transportation. 9% work at home. For most La Jollans,
the commute to work takes between 10 and 24 minutes. 666 lucky
residents have a commute of less than 5 minutes one way.

Not long before his death, Raymond Chandler wrote: "I have lived my life on the edge of nothing." He loved his wife Cissy dearly, and when she passed away on a Sunday in December, Chandler lost it. He loved her so deeply that a month after her death, he wrote a friend: "For thirty years, ten months and four days, she was the light of my life, my whole ambition. Anything else I did was just the fire for her to warm her hands at." She was 18 years older than him, and had been hospitalized repeatedly with pneumonia. Heartbroken, Chandler became acutely depressed and fell back on one of his old habits: drinking heavily.

One evening - or was it during the day? Everything is so nebulous that no one seems to recall very precisely... One day, Chandler was in the bathroom of his La Jolla house. It was on a Tuesday in February, two months and two weeks or so after Cissy died. Chandler had been drinking a lot that day, and he had found a gun that hadn't been used for years. Inconsolable and depressed, he decided he had had enough, and turned the gun on himself. "Fortunately as I now see things," he later wrote, the gun "was loaded with old and probably decomposed ammunition...which just went phutt." Chandler surrendered the gun when the police arrived.

After spending some time under psychiatric observation, he went on with his life. He sold the La Jolla house on 6005 Camino de la Costa, which he had bought for $40,000 in 1946 and where he, Cissy, and their black Persian cat Taki had lived in an almost secluded way. He traveled back to New York and London, started drinking again and fell sorely in love with several women around him, among them Louise Landis Loughner, Helga Greene and Natasha Spender. However, he returned to La Jolla alone, developed pneumonia and died on a Thursday in March, at Scripps clinic. He was buried a few days later at Mount Hope Cemetery. *17* people attended the funeral.

It took some time before Chandler's books received the critical acclaim they deserved, but they now firmly live on. *The Big Sleep* in particular, his first novel, with its lurid, nightmarish vision of Los Angeles, slowly established itself as a new landmark, a monument in American detective fiction. His intimate style and realist technique have been admired and imitated by hundreds of writers after him. And the simple voice of his detective hero, Philip Marlowe, seems to linger sometimes among us like an everlasting echo. *On the way downtown I stopped at a bar and had a couple of double scotches. They didn't do me any good. All they did was make me think of Silver-Wig, and I never saw her again.*

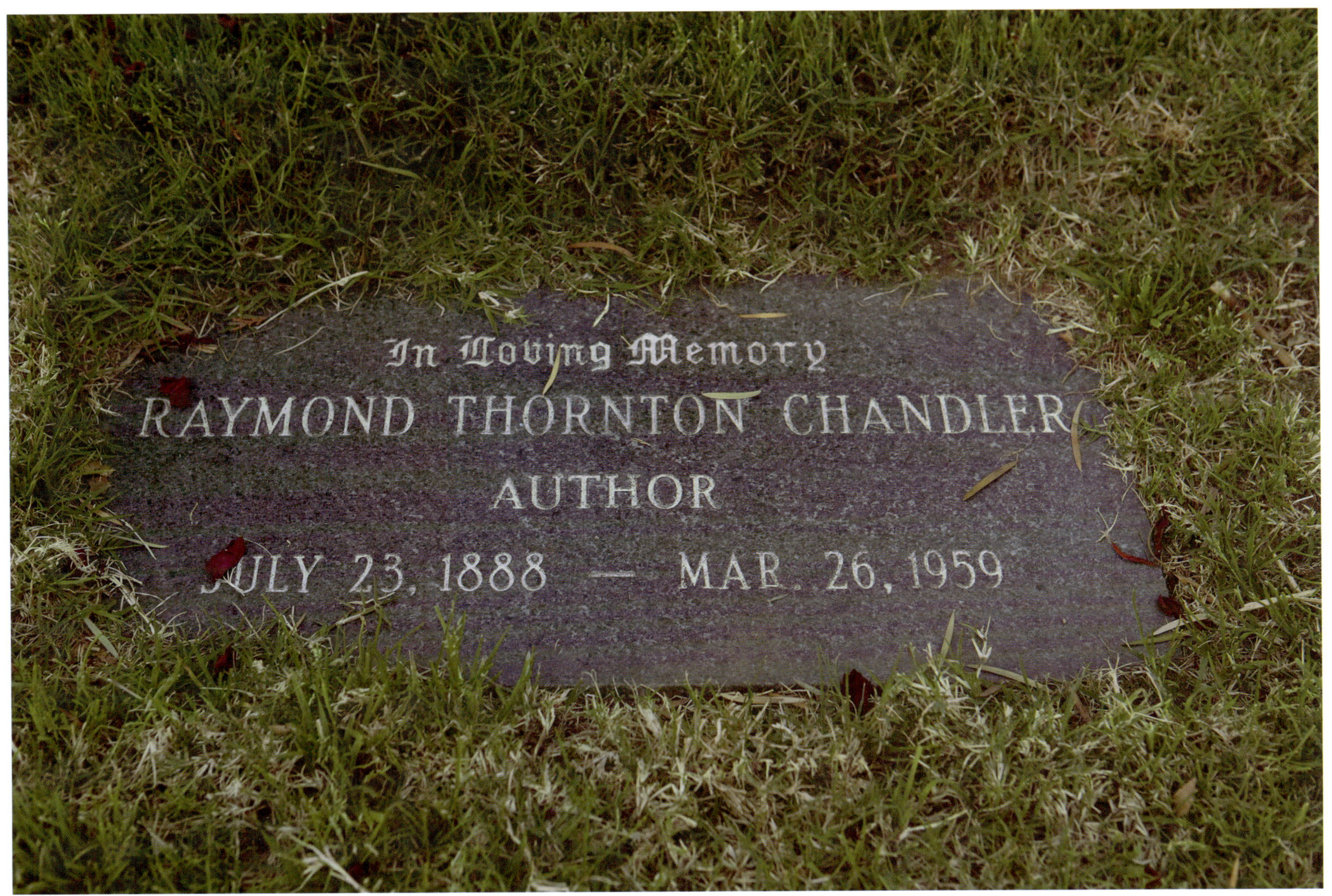
In Loving Memory
RAYMOND THORNTON CHANDLER
AUTHOR
JULY 23, 1888 — MAR. 26, 1959

Strolling in the village of La Jolla is a rich pleasure at all times of the day, but especially so in the morning when the air is crisp and the generous if disciplined vegetation breathes so blissfully. Church bells begin to ring in the distance. Two retired ladies in white shorts and golf-caps walk leisurely towards Seal Beach, the Museum of Contemporary Art and the bells. The allure of their surroundings seems to fascinate them and they wander through it wide-eyed, as though discovering a southern French or Italian village. They may be newcomers at one of many retirement houses in the area, such as Casa de Mañana, by the pier. Or they may just be tourists from out of state.

Around Bishop School and the surrounding church towers, the profusion of older, thicker palm-trees and the Spanish colonial architecture of the churches effortlessly conjure the feeling of drifting into a blessed and delightful oasis, an escape from the desert of banks and chain-stores surrounding it. As they draw nearer, the beautiful, memorable sound of the bells reaches the two entranced explorers more distinctly. It is coming from the *16* chimes up in the tower of St. James Episcopalian church, and it blends delightfully with the screams and laughter of children drifting out of the cheerful La Jolla Recreation Center next door.

Inside the perfectly maintained church and offices of St. James by the Sea, Steven Townsend, Pastor for Music Ministries, wearing a welcoming smile and intelligent eyes, knows well the story of these bells. They date back to 1929 and are the only real bells in La Jolla. Sixteen years ago when he came to La Jolla, the bells rang every 15 minutes, from 9 a.m. to 9 p.m. It was certainly beautiful and evocative of other lands, but it was also a bit too much for the neighborhood. They fell into disrepair, and after their restoration in 2007 the bells became more respectful of the community's desire for tranquility.

Now they don't bother anybody too late in the evening, or too early in the morning. The chimes ring from 10 a.m. to 5 p.m. every day, just as they might in that southern French or Italian village – albeit one with restricted business hours. The two ladies, now utterly enraptured, pause for a moment and close their eyes. They breathe in the perfectly tempered southern Californian atmosphere, enriched at present by the echo of the bells. Then they go on with their stroll, confident that later this evening they will also be able to enjoy a good night of peaceful, chime-free sleep.

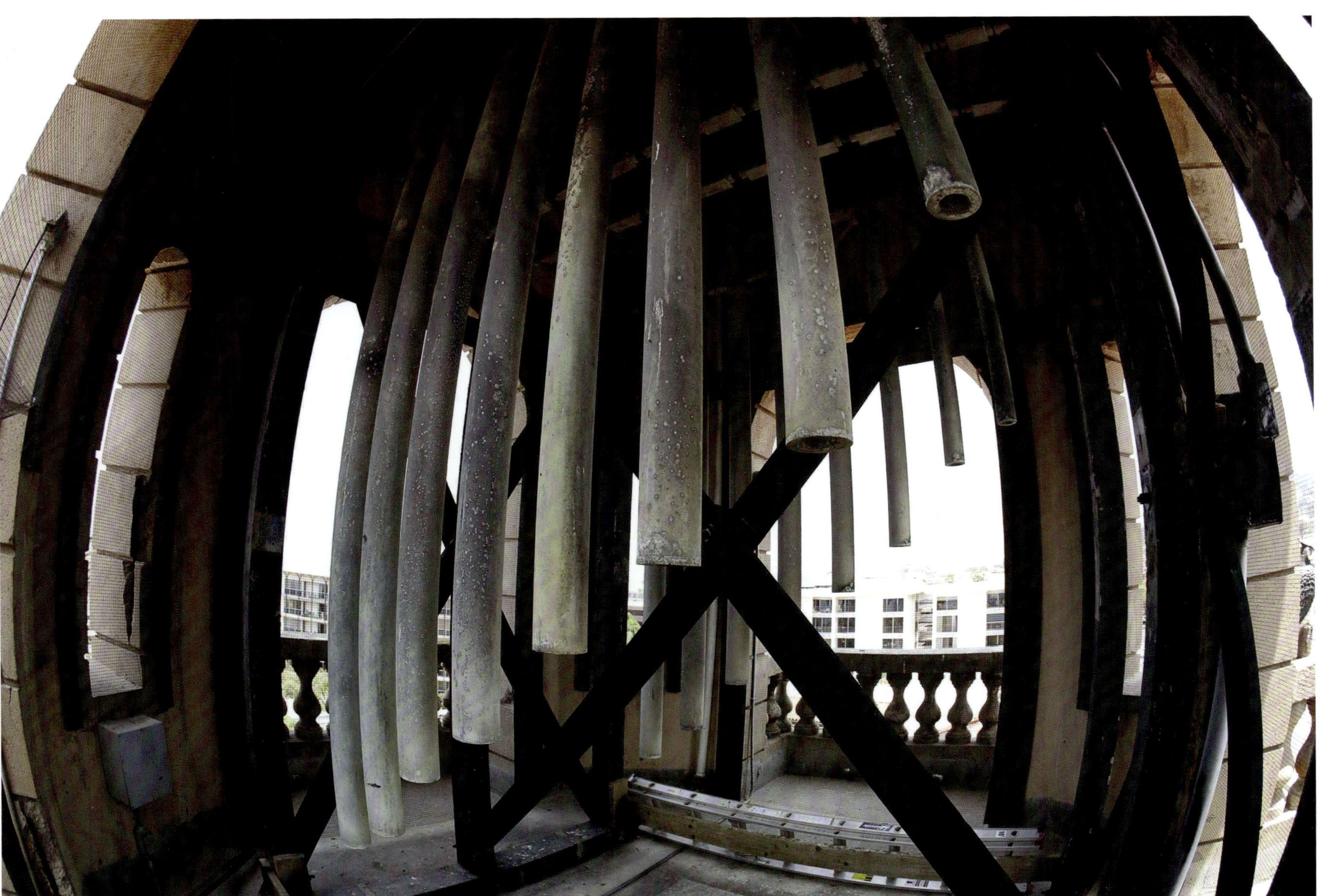

Early on a Saturday evening, the surroundings of Mary, Star of the Sea seem eerily quiet and solemn to the eyes of curious passers-by, dressed up for the evening. But then, when no car is passing, they hear it: a chorus of warm hallelujahs, reaching from inside the church all the way out to the sidewalk. Deep voices sing together, happy to be part of the most popular Spanish-only mass in La Jolla. On the steps by the entrance, a very young mother rocks her baby in her arms. Another Latino mother with at least five kids aged five to twelve passes by almost giddily, as if drinking in the twilit air filled with the unison of singing voices.

Mary, Star of the Sea is a Catholic church on busy Girard Avenue, encircled by banks, design stores and restaurants. Its white, colonial-style edifice, separated from the usual flow of luxurious cars by a garden of cute mini palm trees and rose bushes, is so small and discreet that it's easy to miss. It was dedicated to the Blessed Virgin in 1937, on the premises of an even older church dedicated in 1909, when La Jolla had no more than 1,000 souls to its name. Ten years later, a parish school was founded on the same grounds. At night, the two stars that frame the wooden door at the church entrance are lit in a way that conjures up images of simpler times. A third star may be seen above the wooden door, in a brightly-colored fresco depicting a skinny Virgin Mary in prayer mode. She walks serenely along the sea, accompanied by two flying angels with oblong faces. The arid mountains in the back could almost be a tribute to this area before the recent era of giant malls, condominium complexes and imported palm trees.

Suddenly the wooden door of the church cracks open, and a Catholic priest in his bright white chasuble releases his assembly of dressy faithful out into the cute mini-garden and onto Girard Avenue. Soon an engaging crowd – boys in their Sunday attire, young girls with black, curly hair, gentlemen in suits and ties, and ladies wrapped in elegant long dresses and all sorts of heady perfumes – is mingling in a swirl of Spanish chatter. Back inside the church of old wood and tiny lights, there are only a couple of parishioners left, cleaning up around the candles. A widow, her face covered with a black veil of delicate lace-work, finishes her prayer. She dips her fingers in the holy water at the door, crosses herself, and finally joins the others outside on busy Girard Avenue.

Little by little, the devotees trickle away, quietly vanishing around street corners toward unseen homes. Come Monday morning, some will be back to hear the 8:00 a.m. mass at Mary, Star of the Sea, *15* minutes before the neighboring and affiliated Stella Maris Academy opens its doors to a few hundred kids, many from European and Latin-American origins. A statue of the Blessed Virgin, painted in bright colors, will be kindly awaiting them in the courtyard when they arrive.

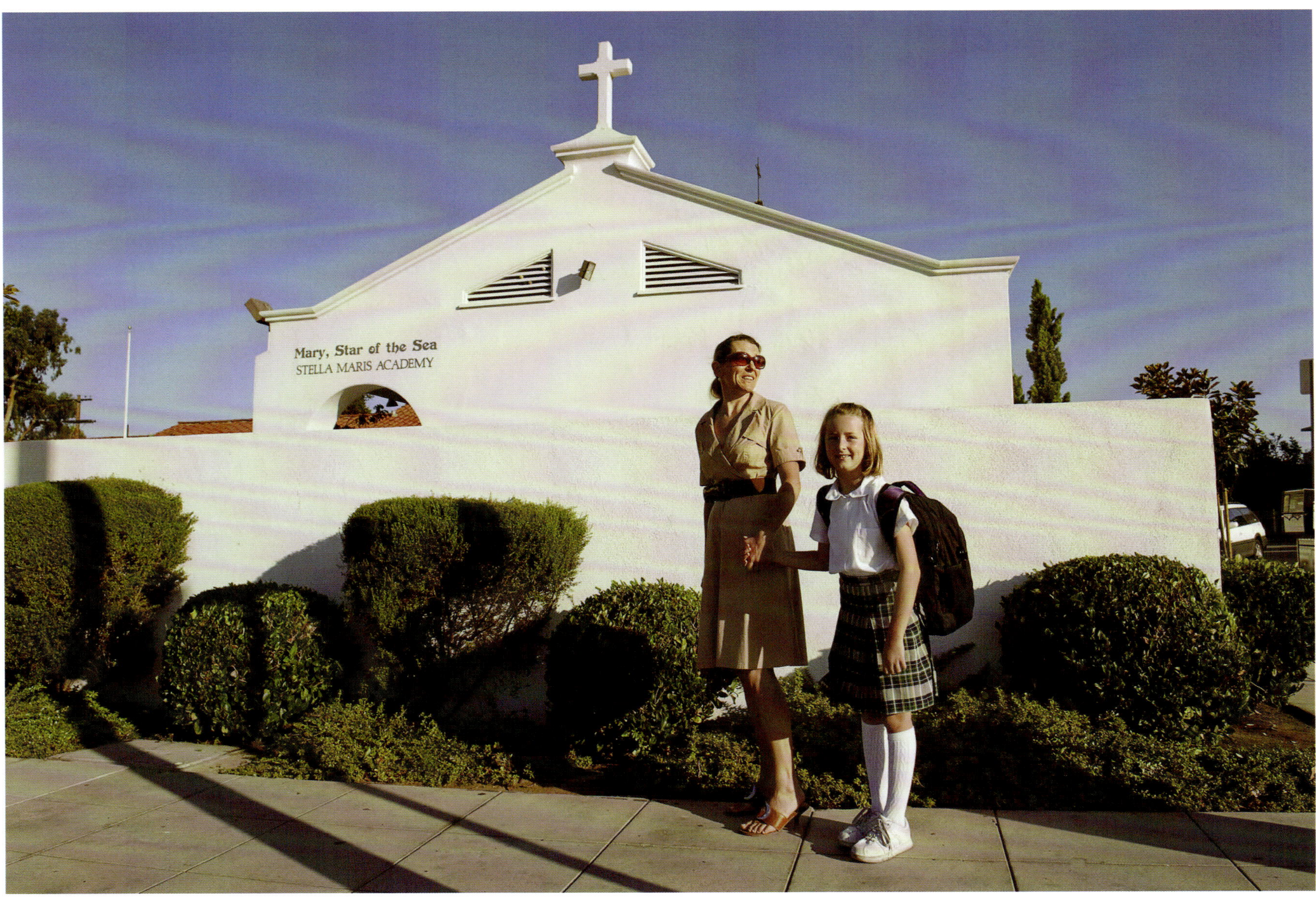

Mary, Star of the Sea
STELLA MARIS ACADEMY

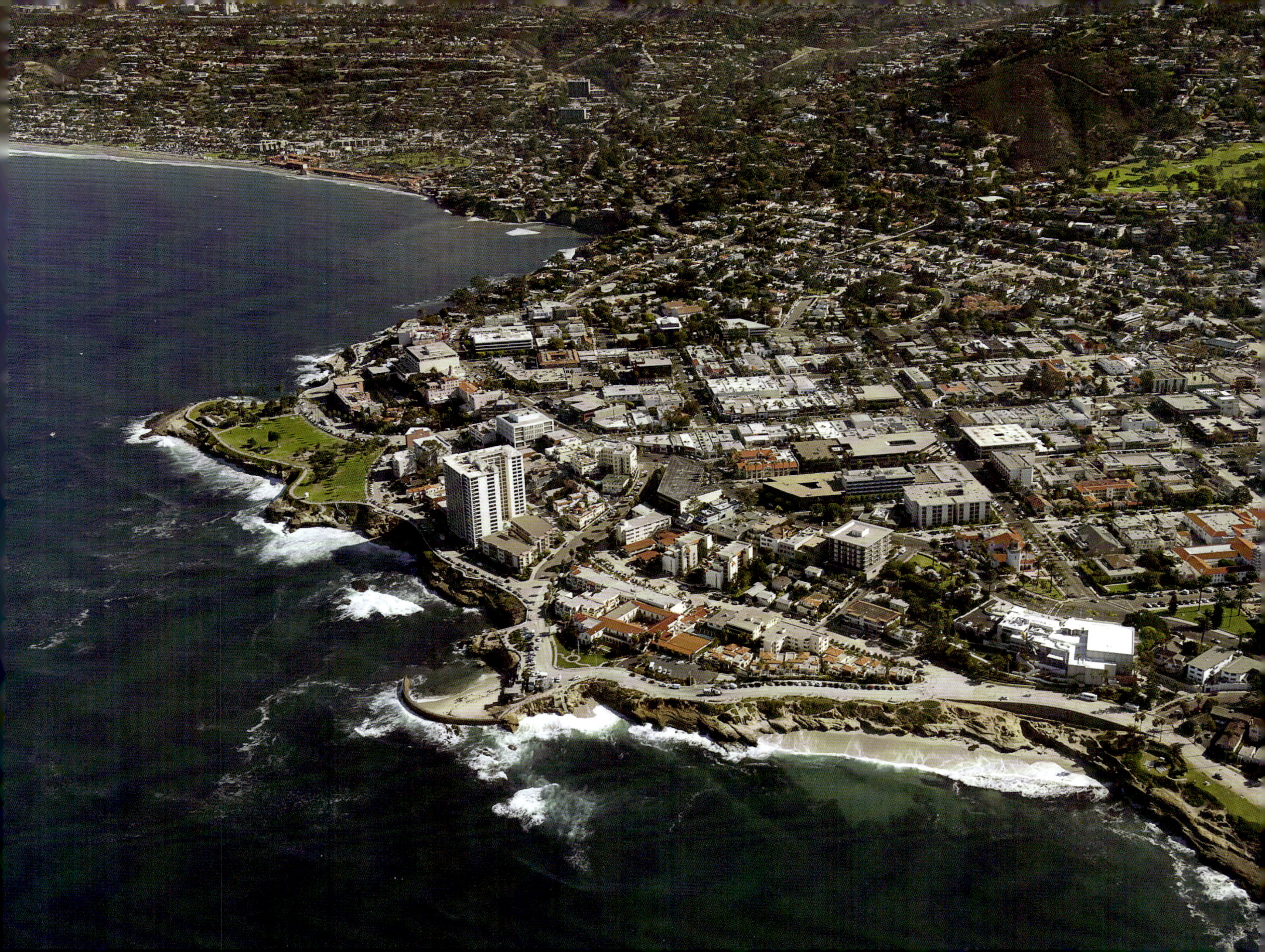

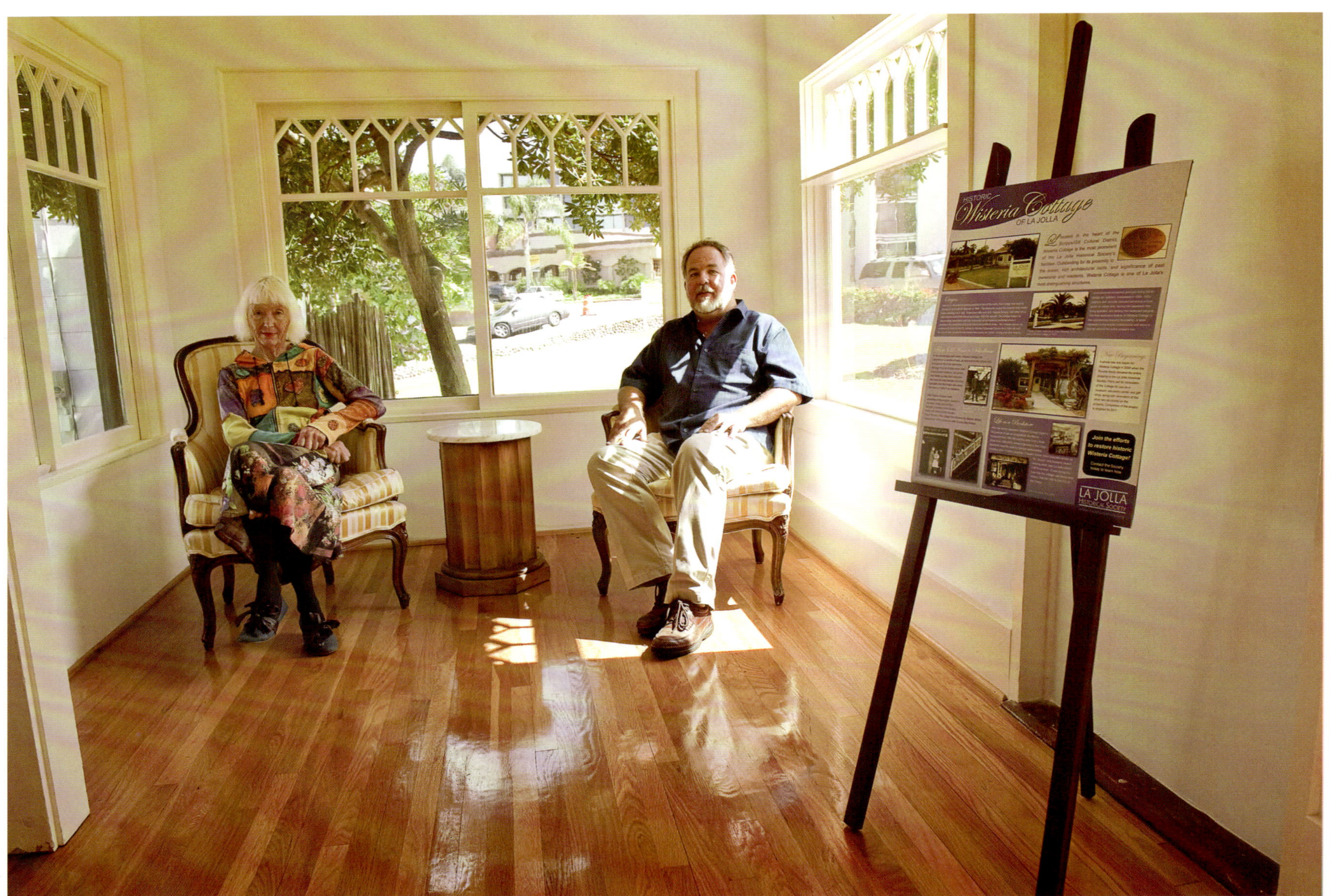

There's a larger crowd than usual at the Historical Society's Wisteria Cottage on Prospect Street. An excited buzz is coming from the charming cottage, and well-dressed ladies flit in and around it like hummingbirds. They're here for the "Secret Garden Tour," happening today as it does each year during the month of May. Ordinary tourists and residents spare them a quizzical glance before returning to the serious business of asking about this particular villa or that burned hotel, a sculptor or a famous tree, the history of this bizarre controversy between the seals and the swimming children or else about a celebrity who lives somewhere in La Jolla during the holidays.

Miss Carol Olten, Historian at the Society, receives these curious locals and tourists alike. Smiling beneath her extravagantly beautiful feathered red hat, she directs them to this or that corner, where 10,000 photographs and files about every house built in La Jolla are within reach, waiting to be researched. Sitting next to her, Michael Mishler, archivist and curator, reserved and bearded, is leafing through the pages of a directory. Carol moved to San Diego in the 60's and promptly fell in love with La Jolla, which she seems to know everything about. A couple of retirees wander in and are enraptured in minutes as Carol spills some of her secrets.

She talks about the decrepit cottages from the 1890's down at the Cove, sitting on land that makes real estate investors salivate at the prospect of millions of dollars of potential profits. She talks about the "house of dreams," an elegant, Chinese-style house built by a lady world-traveler on the slopes of Mount Soledad. She talks about the extravagant, oriental-looking Taj Mahal on Torrey Pines, and about the Green Dragon Colony – the original community of La Jolla artists at the turn of the last century. It used to cost 75 cents for a return ticket from San Diego to La Jolla, an adventure that lured plenty of 19th century tourists to the Cove for a beach picnic. She talks about Max Miller and Raymond Chandler, and even more passionately about Niki de Saint Phalle, for whom she used to design original lamp shades. Then she mentions the Secret Garden Tour...Will they join the little crowd of well-dressed house watchers?

An hour later and a few blocks away from the main cottage, small groups of more or less dressed-up socialites (plus two last-minute retirees), some with impressive, flowery hats, others in baseball caps, ceremoniously enter the first house on this year's Secret Garden Tour. It's one of the most amazing and best-preserved houses in La Jolla: the Darlington House, built in the 1920's by world-traveler and founder of the La Jolla Musical Arts Society Sybil Emma Darlington. Inside, a discreet pianist is playing Chopin. On page *14* of the booklet provided by the Historical Society, the bright-eyed group learns that the remarkable tiles, urns, ornamental grilles and marble columns in the garden were imported from Spain, or from Italy, or even from Greece. The clear sound of a fountain and a few lost seagulls provide background ambience while gracious volunteers for the La Jolla Historical Society stand in the garden and inside the house, ready to answer all their questions.

The Thiele Family in front of their design
studio on Girard Avenue.

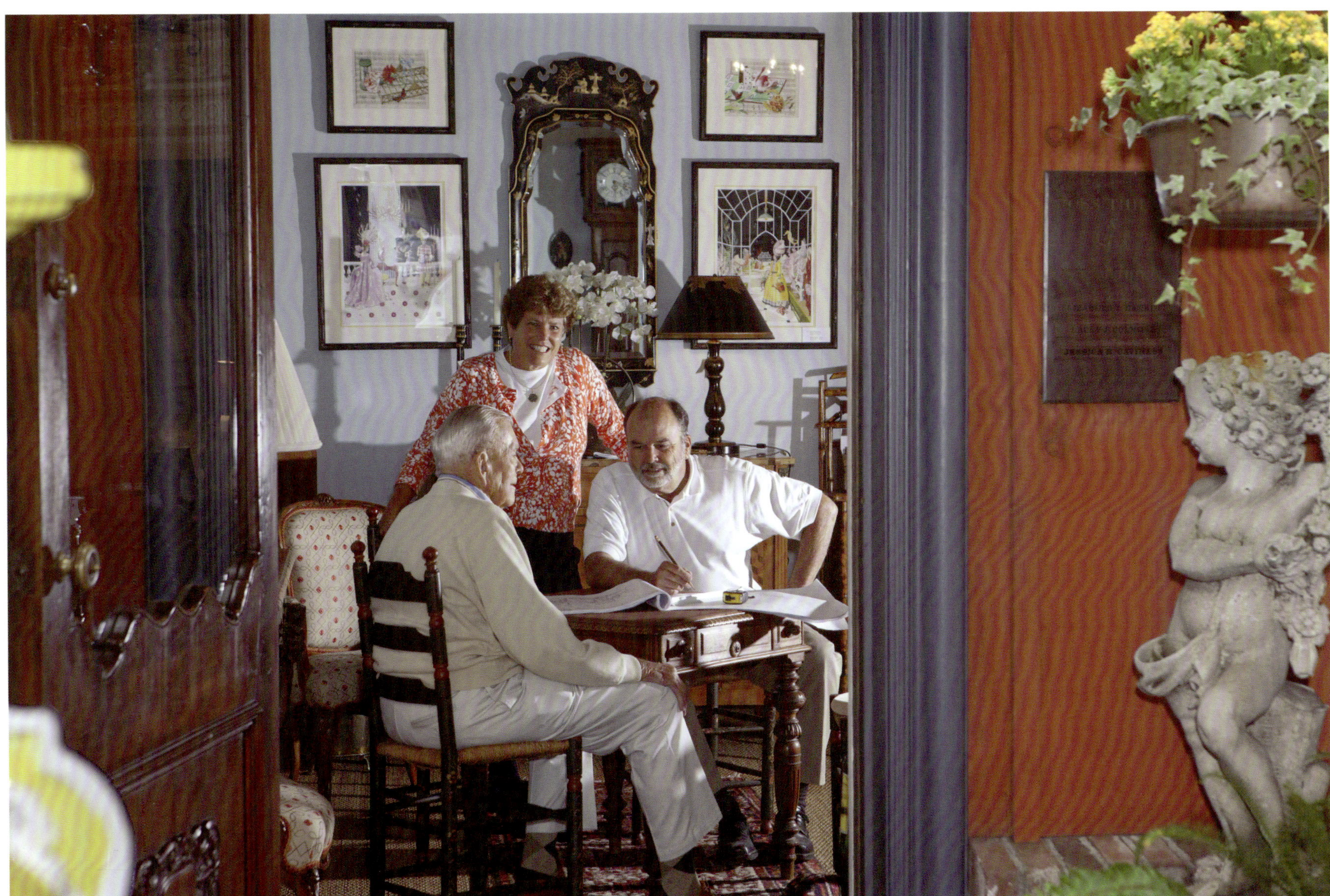

According to Hillary Bo Fellows, who has been a La Jolla resident all his life, La Jolla is the most boring place on earth, but one you can never leave. Bo sits on a bench in the garden of the wood cottage house where he's still living, next to some of his *13* antique cars. He and his friend Bill can talk for hours on this bench. Today, entertaining two outsiders working on a book about the neighborhood, they reminisce about the old days in La Jolla. Mostly their favorite memories are from the 60's, when they used to watch people ride their horses along Torrey Pines road. Christmas parades livened up Friday nights, sometimes becoming too riotous. They talk about the mini hippie revolution down at the Cove, two years before the Summer of Love in San Francisco. A lot changed in the 70's, they say. Lots of new people started coming to La Jolla and then everybody, it seemed, was from Chicago. They narrate all this laughing and sighing alternately.

Bo used to be a fashion model in Milan, Italy. He's lived many years in this house, partying like there was no tomorrow. "This house here has seen a lot of La Jolla history," says Bo impishly. "Everybody partied here and hundreds of girls lost their virginity!" A placid Buddha looks at him from the balcony.

Bo's brother, now deceased, was part of the gang of extreme party-people that inspired Tom Wolfe's novel *The Pump House Gang*, which had a cult following in the surf sub-culture. His mother, a renowned medium, was known as the "white witch of La Jolla" and is remembered fondly by all sorts of people. She died in 1999, but her spirit is said to haunt Bo's house to this day.

Apart from his three enigmatic cats, the most beautiful and ferocious of which he brought back from Mexico, Bo is proudest of his collection of thirteen antique cars.

They're mostly American and repainted in eye-catching pastel colors. He has them parked in his backyard and all over the neighboring blocks. There's no question that he could sell some of them for a small fortune. But, throwing them a last glance before he heads back into the house, Bo dismisses that idea. He just isn't ready to part with his "babies."

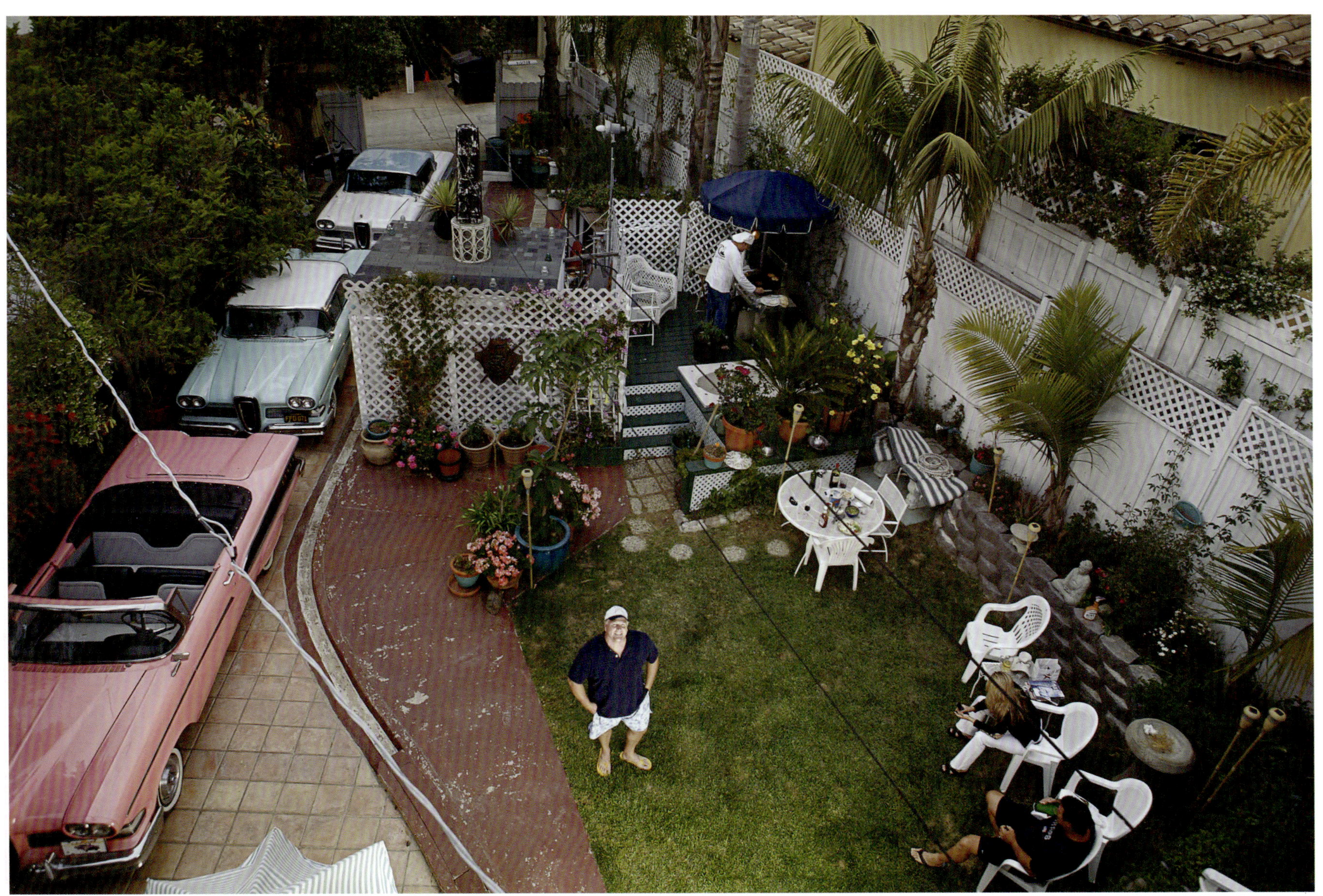

On what is for some the most beautiful Saturday night of the year, hundreds of very elegant couples are arriving more or less ceremoniously at the La Jolla Beach and Tennis Club. A slightly strange young lady, dressed in a long, black, stylish and rather provocative dress with a headband and a feather on top of her head, is greeting everybody at the gate, playing absently with the feather boa wrapped around her neck and all her body as she does so. For the distinguished guests who are just arriving, it is apparent that tonight will be a special one. The month of August has just begun, and its warm evenings are longer than at any other time of the year.

Tonight the Club looks more exclusive than ever. The parade of evening gowns and tuxedos rivals that of the antique auto-mobiles, some adorned with gorgeous flowers and young models dressed in prohibition-era costumes, some touring the parking lot with prominent VIPs on their backseats. Everybody smiles indulgently at one another, and it only takes a moment to be swept away into the cacophony of conversation, music, laughter, and delicate and abundant food, all mingled with fine wines and liquors that are clearly appreciated by the array of bedecked La Jollans, some in elaborate costumes. This is the 62nd edition of the Jewell Ball, and this year's theme, "Speakeasy," evokes nebulous memories of the secret and decadent parties of the roaring 20's.

A glittering lady in a clear, gleaming gown moves with cheerful ease from guest to guest, as if dancing. She could be the queen of the night, and in a way she is. Her name is Barbara Mullingan, and this year she is the affable and energetic President of *Las Patronas*, a group of 50 committed women that has helped more than 100 beneficiaries and distributed more than $12 million in grants in its 62-year history. Health, education, social services and cultural arts: that's where the money raised by these lavish Jewell Balls goes to. But now is not the time to calculate figures. "There is no room for big, conventional speeches at the Jewell Ball," Barbara says. "This is the most beautiful night of the year in La Jolla, and all the guests who are fortunate enough to be part of it are going to be free to enjoy it the way they wish. Go on, enjoy the music." Behind her, three orchestras are tuning up simultaneously.

As if instructed by a secret language of thoughts from the night's hostess, one of them immediately begins to play louder in the adjacent, magnificent ballroom under the stars. The night is young, but already an elegant younger couple is dancing, oddly solemn and seemingly in heaven. Barbara is gliding away towards some other fortunate guests dressed as Al Capone's gang, surrounded by the smell of grilled meats and expensive perfumes.

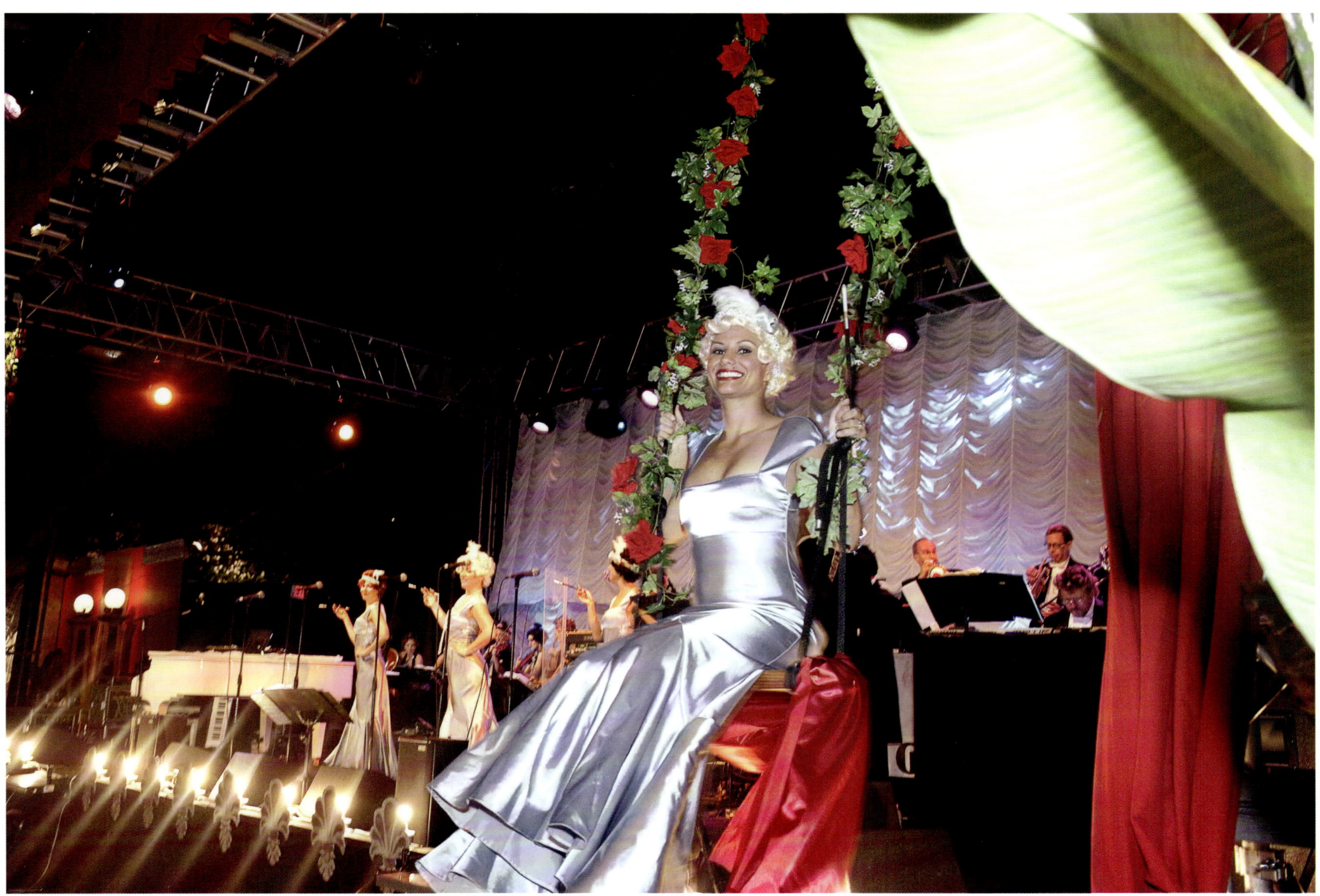

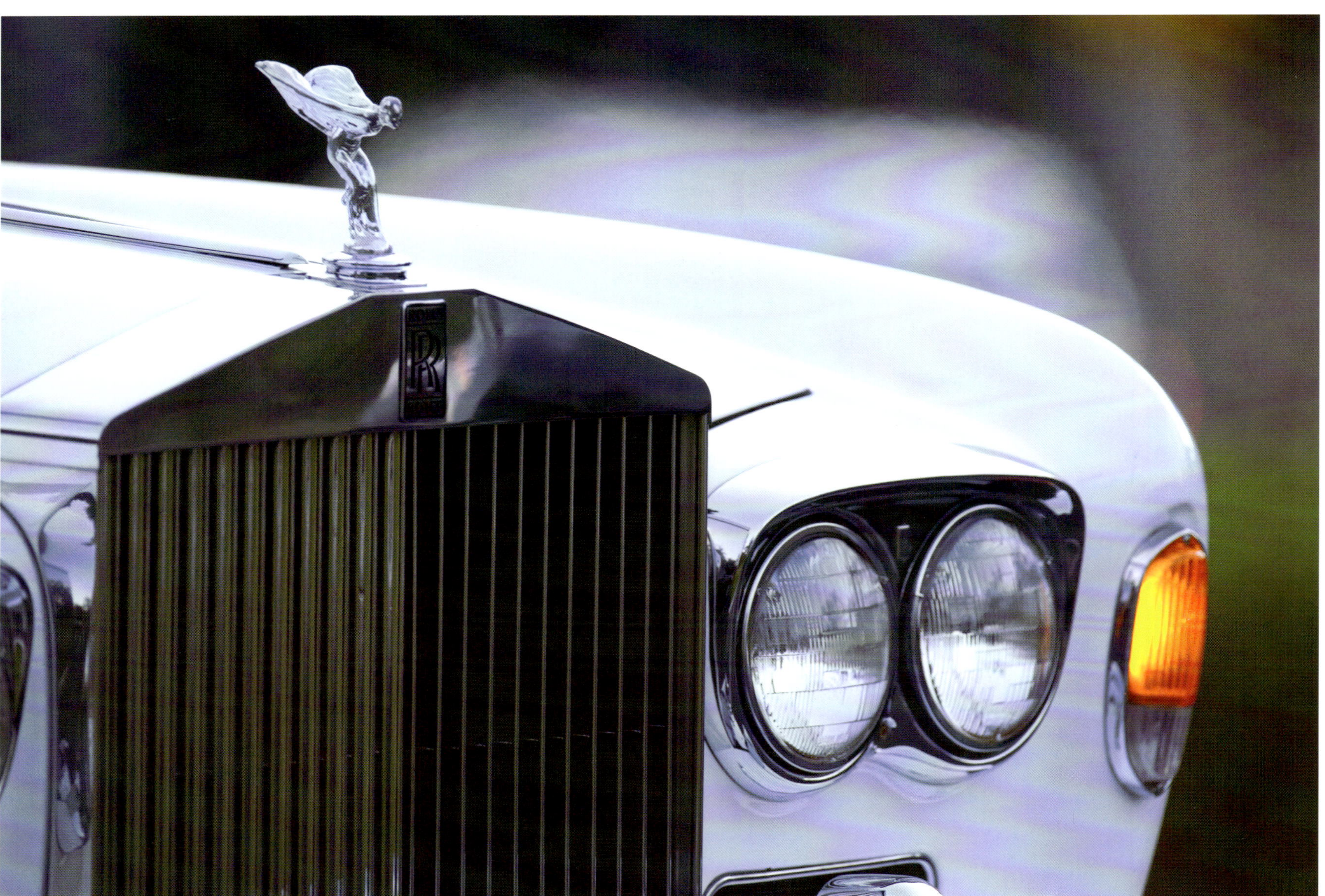

There are
about 22 branches of
banks in the village of
La Jolla: 6 on Girard Avenue, 5 on Ivanhoe,
3 on Prospect, and 2 on Wall Street. The top
industry in the zip code is Research and Development in the
Physical, Engineering, and Life Sciences, with around 4,000
employees. Tourism, including hotels and restaurants is the second
largest industry. In 1850, two brothers by the name of Samuel and
Daniel Sizer purchased 2 pueblo lots of 80 acres for $1.25 an acre, and
over the next 19 years the population of these La Jolla land plots began to
grow. By the late 20th century, the same plots were worth 1,000,000 times
more than what they had been valued at in 1869, selling at a minimum of
$1,250,000 per acre. In the early years of the new millennium, the
median home price in La Jolla was $964,134, and the median
household income was $74,700 per year. When they retire,
La Jollans may choose to live at the Casa de Mañana
retirement community, where monthly fees
range from $2,700 for a studio apartment
to $9,600   for the most
luxurious two   bedroom villa.

When you first meet Jane it's difficult to determine her age: she has wrinkles all over her young face, a shy smile, long blonde and grey hair, and gentle, light blue eyes. She's been living on the street for about a year and half, timidly begging for money to survive. "Very few people would take the time to be rude to me," she says. What she gets most often is $1. On holidays, people become more generous, offering food and sometimes lodging. So far, one thing that they have never offered her is flowers.

Jane wears blue jeans, white tennis shoes, and a light blue sweatshirt with the number *11* on it. She likes to go to cafés and sit on the terrace, watching people walk by. She also likes to read the New York Times. Usually, she reads the front page, the business section, and the arts section. She doesn't want to be photographed because she's afraid that her mother might see her on a newspaper. Jane arrived in San Diego in 1986 after growing up in the Midwest. She was working in the real estate business when, one day, she became seriously ill. She didn't have proper medical coverage and she lost her job. Before long she found herself on the street, unable to afford doctors and hospitals. Now, Jane has to wait to become sick to the point of not being able to breathe before an ambulance will come to pick her up and take her to Scripps Hospital. That has happened about ten times in the last six months, she says.

Jane was living in La Jolla before her illness and she likes the area, so she's not going anywhere else. It's safer, less stressful than other neighborhoods, she says. She estimates the number of regular street people in the village to be about a dozen, among which three are women. "We're like old friends, protecting and helping each other," she says. She loves flowers. She loves the library, where she can spend more than two hours a day. On Thursdays, when it's free, she visits the museum. She likes to take bus 30 to Albertsons, where she buys fruits and veggies, trying to avoid fast food chains. "I'll probably die of a heart attack soon," she says, "but I dream about finding a job in a flower shop one day."

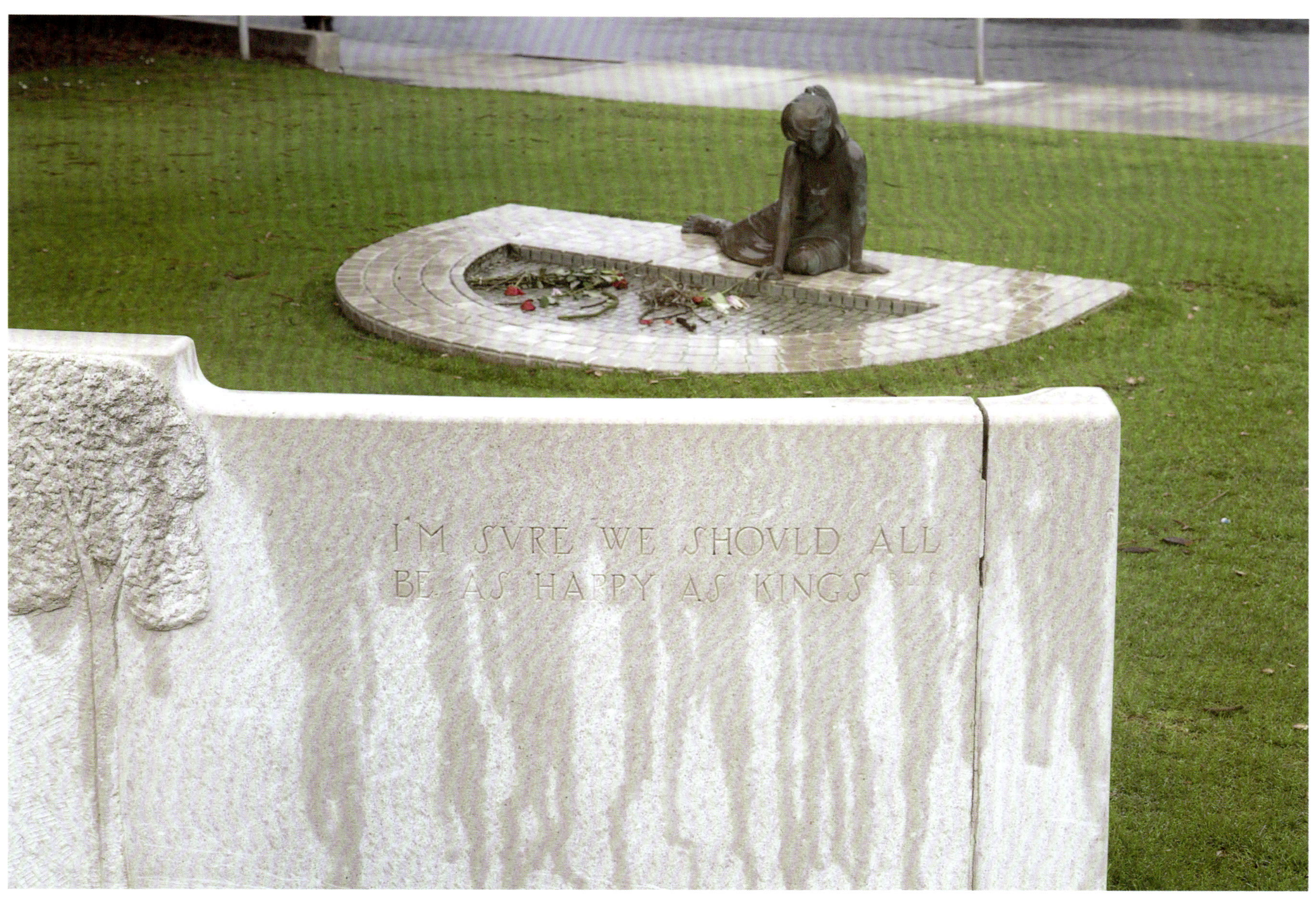

I'M SVRE WE SHOVLD ALL
BE AS HAPPY AS KINGS

In a rocky habitat couched between the intertidal zone and the edge of the continental shelf, in the depths of the dark ocean, they are lurking. Centuries ago, the abundance of spines on their backs, their *10* legs and their dark, hard protective exoskeleton won them worshippers among the Moche people of ancient Peru. With their round, fixed and quietly stubborn eyes they can glare at you for hours, and you don't know what to say or do. They may live to be 100 years old. Rumor has it that, if they are able to escape injury or captivity, they can live indefinitely. And they never stop growing.

They are nocturnal, hiding in the rocks by day and hunting down smaller, weaker creatures at night, eating them alive. If need be, they may also feed themselves on dead organic matter and, when reduced to captivity, they may even resort to cannibalism. Their blood is blue, and they shed their skin during molting, a period of vulnerability for them, during which they may change color, and after which they always feel compelled to eat their own forsaken membrane. They are not social beings; on the contrary, they often deliberately choose to live apart from their kinfolk. It is in the gloomiest crevices that they seem to revel most. The question of whether or not they can experience pain still remains unresolved.

They're here in La Jolla, and they're branded as "spiny," though they lack the large claws of their eastern cousins. They are known to attack slow-moving animals, and sometimes they migrate *en masse*. During their journey, they use their long antennae to stay together by contact and produce loud, harsh sounds to repel predators, rubbing the base of their antennae against a file. These sounds have been compared by some to the whine of a bowing violin string. However, when healthy, they move away from the diseased, leaving them to fend for themselves. The most courageous of local humans catch them live with bare hands in the Cove on winter nights, and soon after plunge them into a large pot of boiling water, where they depart this life that could have never ended and become, during the five month long "season," a delicate gastronomic delight.

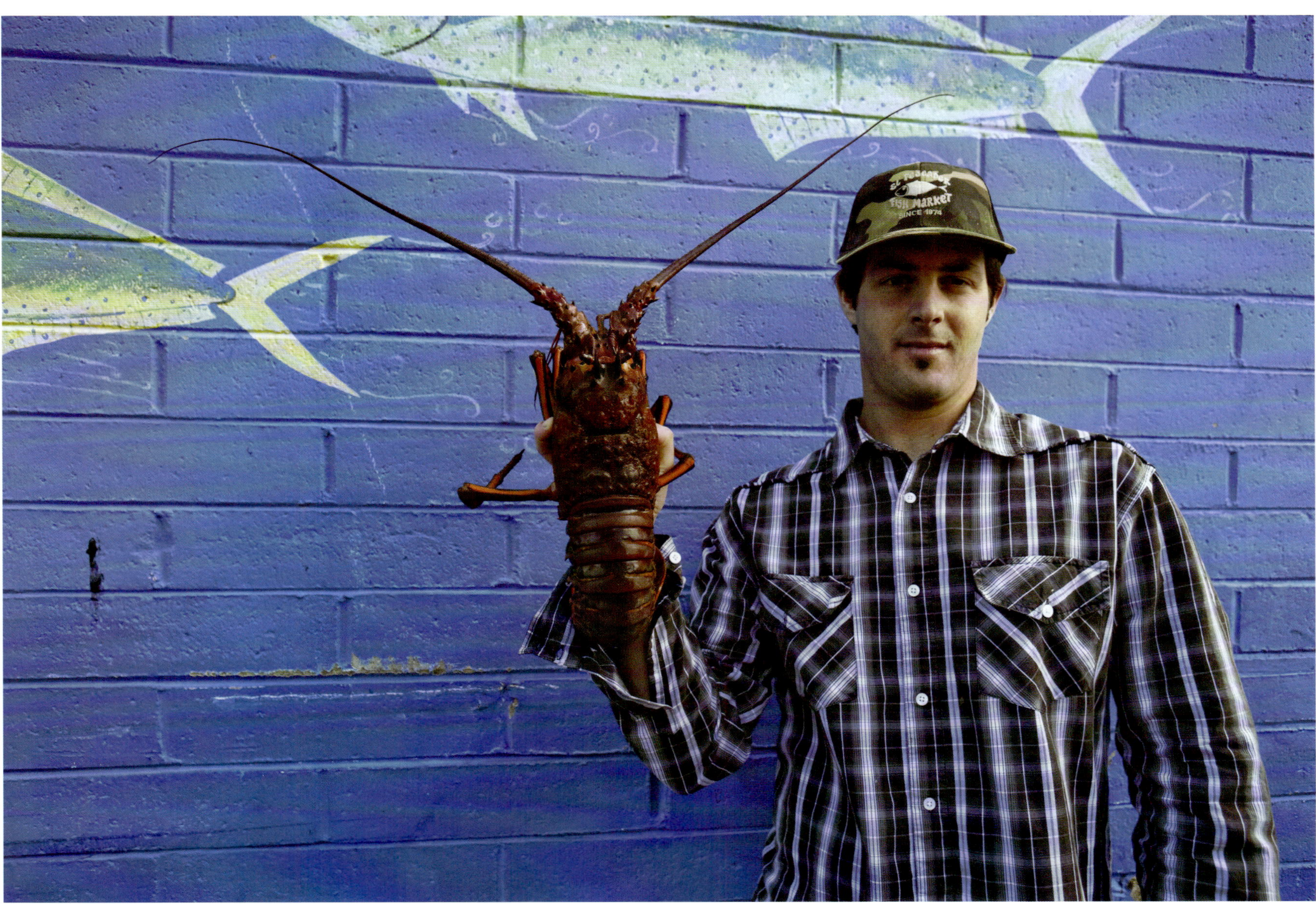

It's a tiny restaurant hidden in a tiny, modern version of an Italian piazza in La Jolla. Only a few tables fit onto the patio, placed right where stray pedestrians can catch a glimpse of who's sitting where and what's on the plates. But however hidden and somewhat difficult to find, *la Dolce Vita* is always crowded on weekends, particularly on Friday night. The singing presence of Luigi Luevano, the self-proclaimed "One and Only" with his large teasing smile and his perfectly trimmed moustache, on the patio and even often at the entrance of the courtyard at 1237 Prospect, may well have something to do with it.

Luigi started his singing career 45 years ago without any formal voice lessons or ability to read music. With two singers for parents, he had always loved singing and when he was drafted into the Army during Vietnam, Luigi ended up performing for the US forces after an avid opera fan, a Lieutenant Colonel, overheard him singing in the Army showers. He now sings every Friday night at the *Dolce Vita*, and jokes around, pretending that every middle-aged man is his "grandson".

Luigi is not that old, and he's not singing alone on the restaurant's patio, gliding from table to table and all the way to the street and back under the cute lights hanging in the tree leaves. Tonight he's accompanied by Chantal, who was born in Morocco and loves to sing Edith Piaf songs, and by Linda, the owner of the store next door who started singing on Fridays after Luigi came into her store with a microphone. Two more singers join them later to follow the pianist Audrey's lead. Some nights, there are *9* of them who take turns singing mostly Italian arias. Opera, operetta.

As the evening goes, *la Dolce Vita* gets more and more crowded and people chat louder, clapping and singing along. Enzo Castiglione, the owner, who is also the chef and a winemaker, is getting ready to play percussion. There is a family of twelve: men, women and kids of all ages and generations gaily sitting at a long and somewhat messy table as if they were in Italy. At other much smaller tables lit by candles, young couples just seem happy to be here, not saying much. Luigi is singing in a playfully seductive manner into the eyes of a charming young blonde with curly hair while a group of Latino students, who seem to be dressed very formally for their age, is waiting for a table, fascinated and shy. In everybody's face there is a combination of excitement and fear that Luigi might come and sing directly into your eyes. If you're particularly lucky, he might even ask you to sing along.

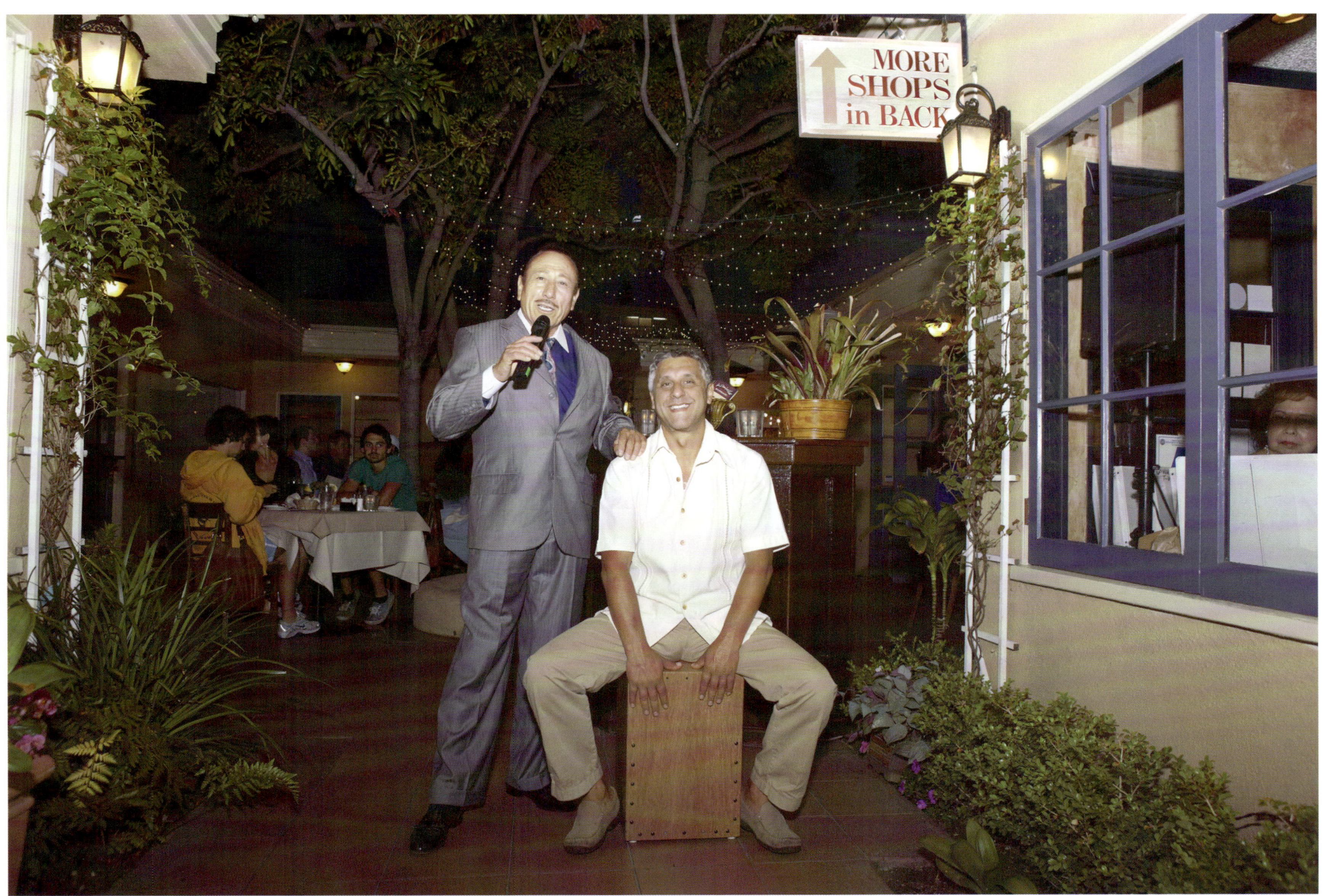

MORE
SHOPS
in BACK

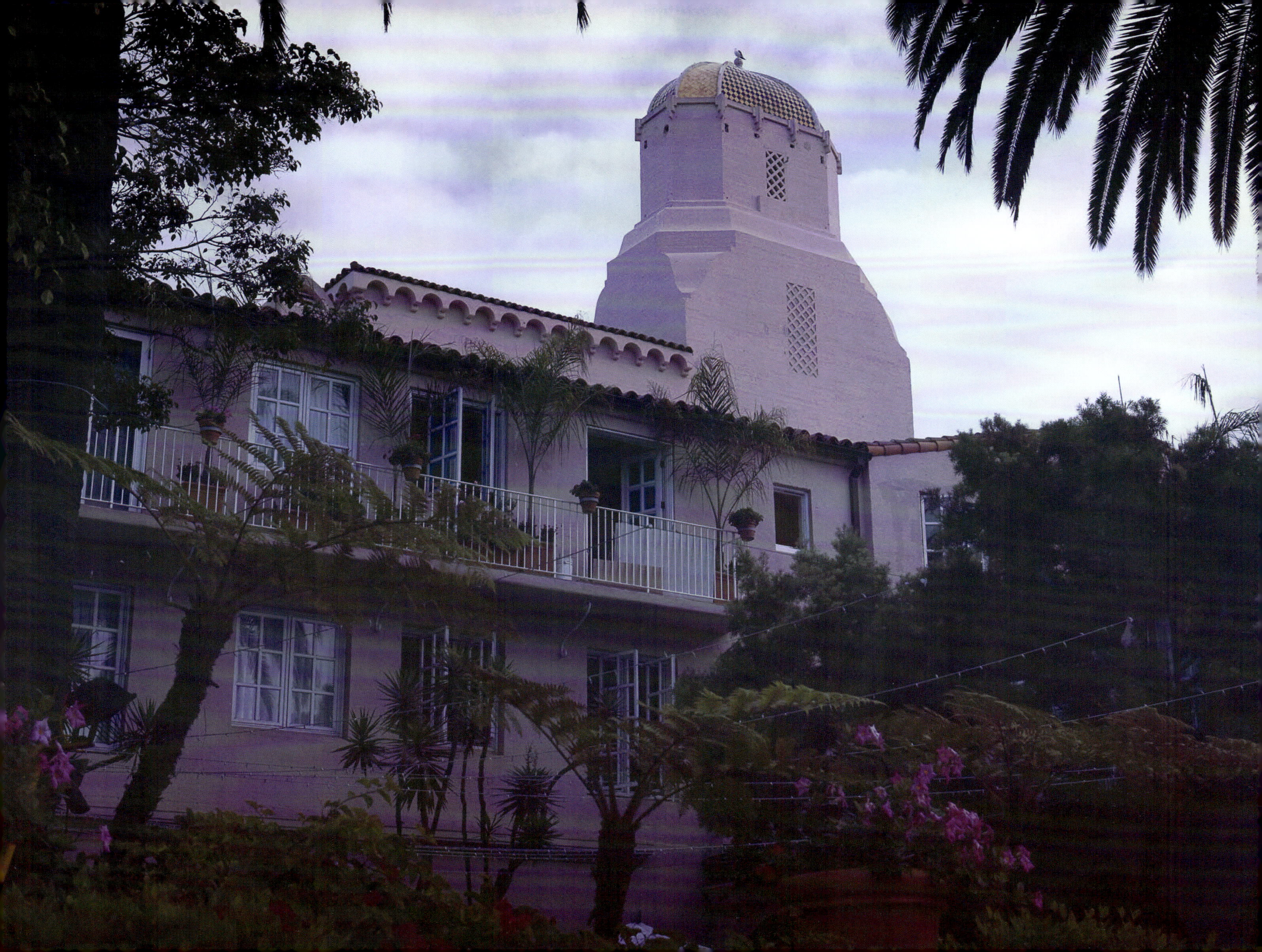

There is more than one way to live the good life in La Jolla. Talking about classy, high-end luxury hotels with impeccable service and gorgeous surroundings by the Cove, two in particular command widespread recognition: *La Valencia*, and the *Grande Colonial*. Both date back to the beginning of the 20th century, and both allow you to liberally spend lots of money in even the shortest of visits.

Entering the "Pink Lady" is like starting a delicious journey into a refined world full of sweet colors and blooming vegetation. The entrance corridor looks like a hedge of foliage extending welcoming arms to you with unquestionable elegance, and there's a delicate and pervasive scent in the air coming from a huge bouquet of pink lilies in the reception hall. A grandiose curtain opens onto the majestic ocean from a grand dining room filled with white tables and candles, but despite the Viennese grandeur, most guests have chosen to sit outside on the wide balcony overlooking the Cove. Couples and families nibble on hors d'oeuvres and enjoy the colors of the evening. Palms, fuchsia bougainvilleas, white camellias, and birds of paradise sprawl everywhere beneath them, their leaves and flowers reflecting in the blue water and bluer Spanish tiles of the pool.

A short walking distance from the Valencia, the *Nine-Ten* restaurant inside the Grande Colonial answers its rival's feast for the eyes with one for the taste buds. Like the Valencia, everything at the Grande Colonial is impeccably nice and luxurious. There are three rare firewalls dating back from 1928 at the entrance of the corridors that lead to the rooms. Enter Nine-Ten and there is a different kind of electricity in the air. It might be coming from the bartender, who is carrying crazily-colored Jell-o shots on a sleek Japanese-style plate to an ecstatic table of dressy women that resembles the cast of *Sex and the City*. Tonight, they get to taste *8* different flavors of Jell-o shots including Mojito, Pomegranate and vodka, and Frangelico. With its warm mahogany wood, contemporary furniture, and a great patio for people-watching on Prospect Street, the restaurant sucks you in immediately. Ross Harmon, the wine director, is from New Orleans, Chef Jason Knibbs is from Jamaica, and you soon find yourself drinking a rare Sauvignon Blanc from Burgundy to accompany a plate of Hamachi sashimi with marinated baby shiitake mushrooms – and that's only the appetizer. It's so incredibly fresh and creative that you have to imagine a new country to categorize it. The entrée is on its way, and you know that resistance is futile. While your tongue is fighting a losing battle against the slow roasted lamb loin, valiantly struggling to return to the real world, Pastry Chef Jack Fisher will quietly be preparing the coup de grâce in a final explosion of rare and intoxicating flavors. Undeniably, affluence has its charms in the village of La Jolla.

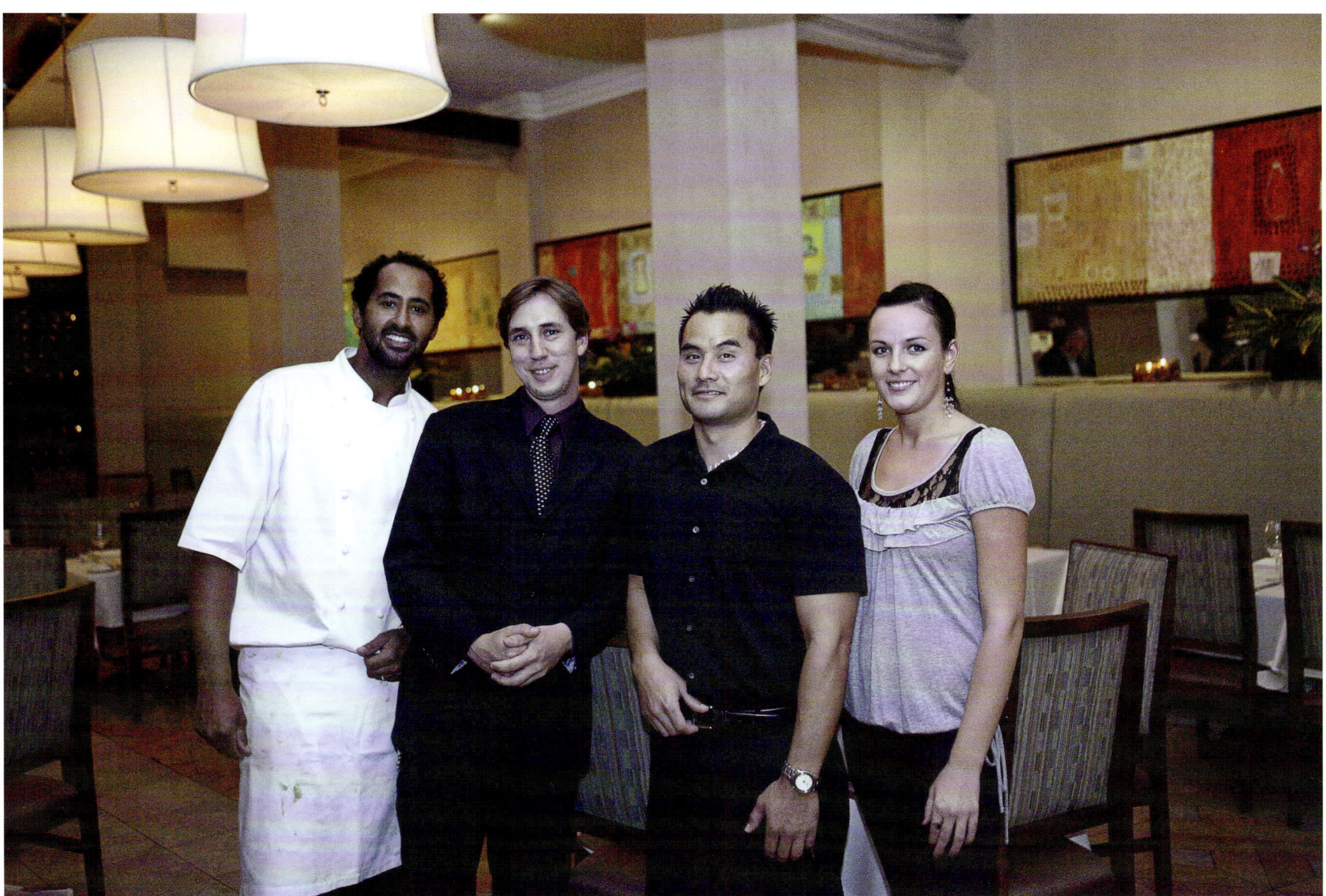

The Athenaeum on Wall Street.

Following Page: Pleasure Point, a Nancy
Rubins' sculpture at the Museum of
Contemporary Art, La Jolla.

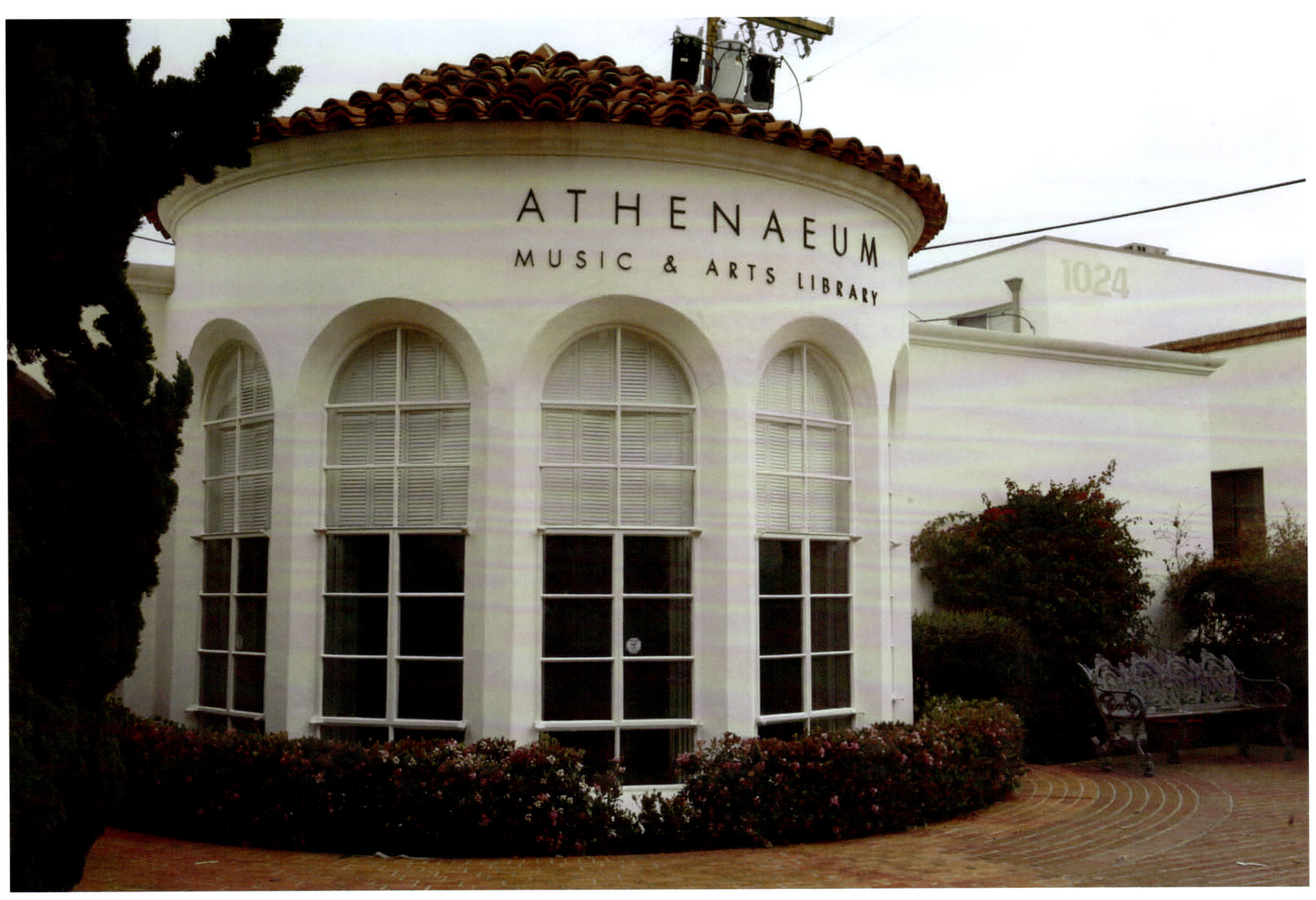

ATHENAEUM
MUSIC & ARTS LIBRARY
1024

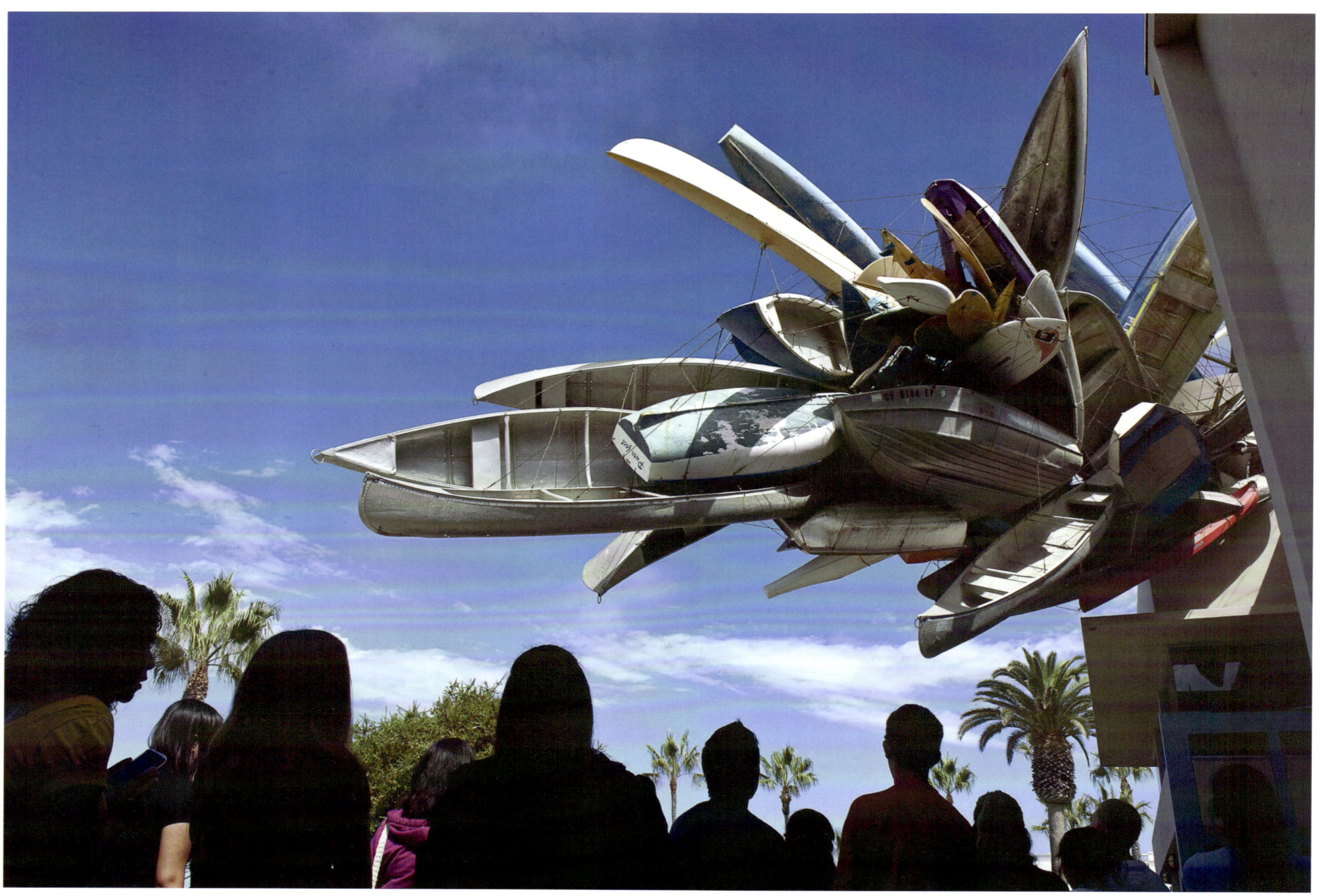

La Jolla Playhouse was founded in 1947 by Gregory Peck, Dorothy McGuire, and Mel Ferrer. It has received more than 300 awards for theatre excellence and currently boasts more than 10,000 subscribers. Numerous Playhouse productions have moved on to Broadway, where they have garnered a total of 29 Tony Awards. The Athenaeum is one of only 17 membership libraries in the United States. Currently, it has 2,300 subscribers. Membership costs $40 a year. To become a founder and gain Patron Member Privileges, you need to donate at least $5,000 to the library. In December 2009, a double cappuccino cost $4.00 at the Museum of Contemporary Art. General admission to the museum is $10. On the 3rd Thursday evening of every month between 5 and 7 pm., admission is free for everyone. It's also free for anyone under 25 years old.

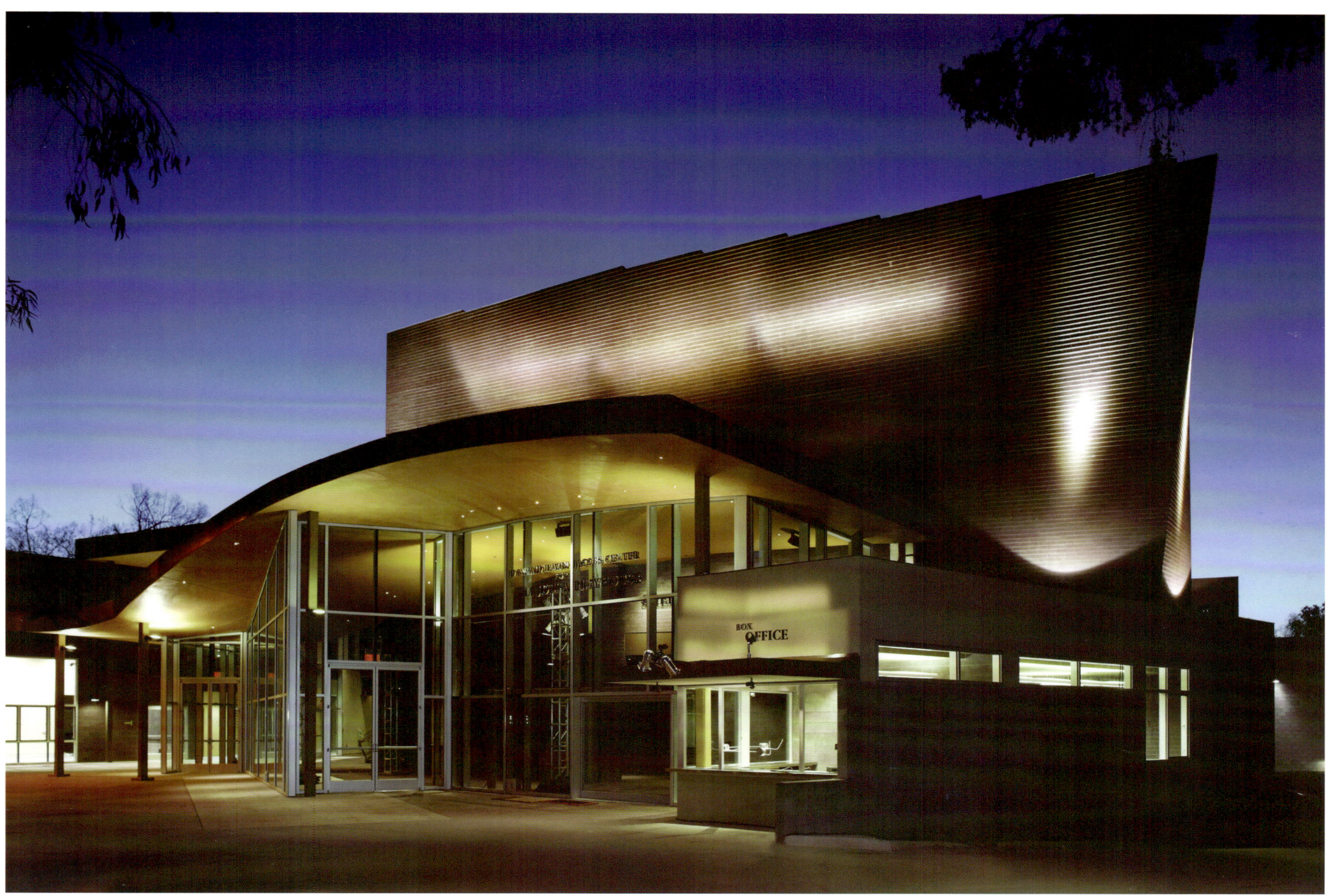

Inside Warwick's bookstore on Girard, there's a good crowd of well-dressed book-worms sitting in a disciplined fashion in front of a microphone, waiting. It's Saturday evening. At this very moment, the sun is sinking sumptuously into the ocean before another somewhat disciplined crowd that never seems to get tired of it. Behind the congregation at Warwick's, the sky is a blur of rapidly changing colors. But nobody's really paying attention. They're here for someone special, and you can feel the intimate bond that a reader develops toward the author of a beloved book humming in the room. Hip-joined couples and old-time friends wearing chic earrings go on with their small talk, a glass of white wine in one hand and some cheese and nuts in the other, their eyes moving from chatting friend to microphone and back again.

W.T. Warwick founded his bookstore in 1896 and relocated it to La Jolla on the eve of World War II by purchasing Redding's store, which had started selling books to La Jollans and tourists alike at the turn of the 20th century, near the entrance to the La Jolla Cave. "La Jolla has always been a good spot for bookstores," Adrian Newell, the book buyer at Warwick's who has been working at the store for 22 years, commented some weeks ago. Sitting next to Adrian, Nancy Warwick, the great-granddaughter of W.T. Warwick and the shop's current owner, smiled. "At one time, there were 7 bookstores here within half a mile!" she added, speaking over the noise of her two white poodles, Milo and Django, as they frantically ran around her office upstairs. A steady stream of people walked up and down the steps, flitting in and out of offices and juggling various books and stationery items. That day, Nancy estimated that Warwick's currently employs between 38 and 45 staff members.

Downstairs, the author has arrived, charming and shy, dressed in a somewhat messy, slightly open shirt with a lazy beard and curly hair. He begins to read the first chapter of his book, entitled *City of Thieves*, the story of two boys looking for a dozen eggs in besieged Leningrad and one of the Warwick's staff favorites. In front of him the audience listens and nods serenely. Immune to the soft-voiced young novelist's account of dead German corpses, famine, danger and misery, children's wood mobiles dance overhead, pushed by the gentle breeze of the air conditioner. Among their ranks are colored sailboats, fancy terrestrial globes, World War I planes, whales, multicolored hot-air balloons, and pelicans. Suddenly the author's young daughter starts singing "happy birthday to you," and he cracks up along with the audience. Everybody has a question for David Benioff, a really good one that has been concocted and carefully kept for weeks. They will have to be stopped at some point if the store wants to close before the middle of the night, but for now the wine is good and the company is better, and ticking clocks are a long, long ways away.

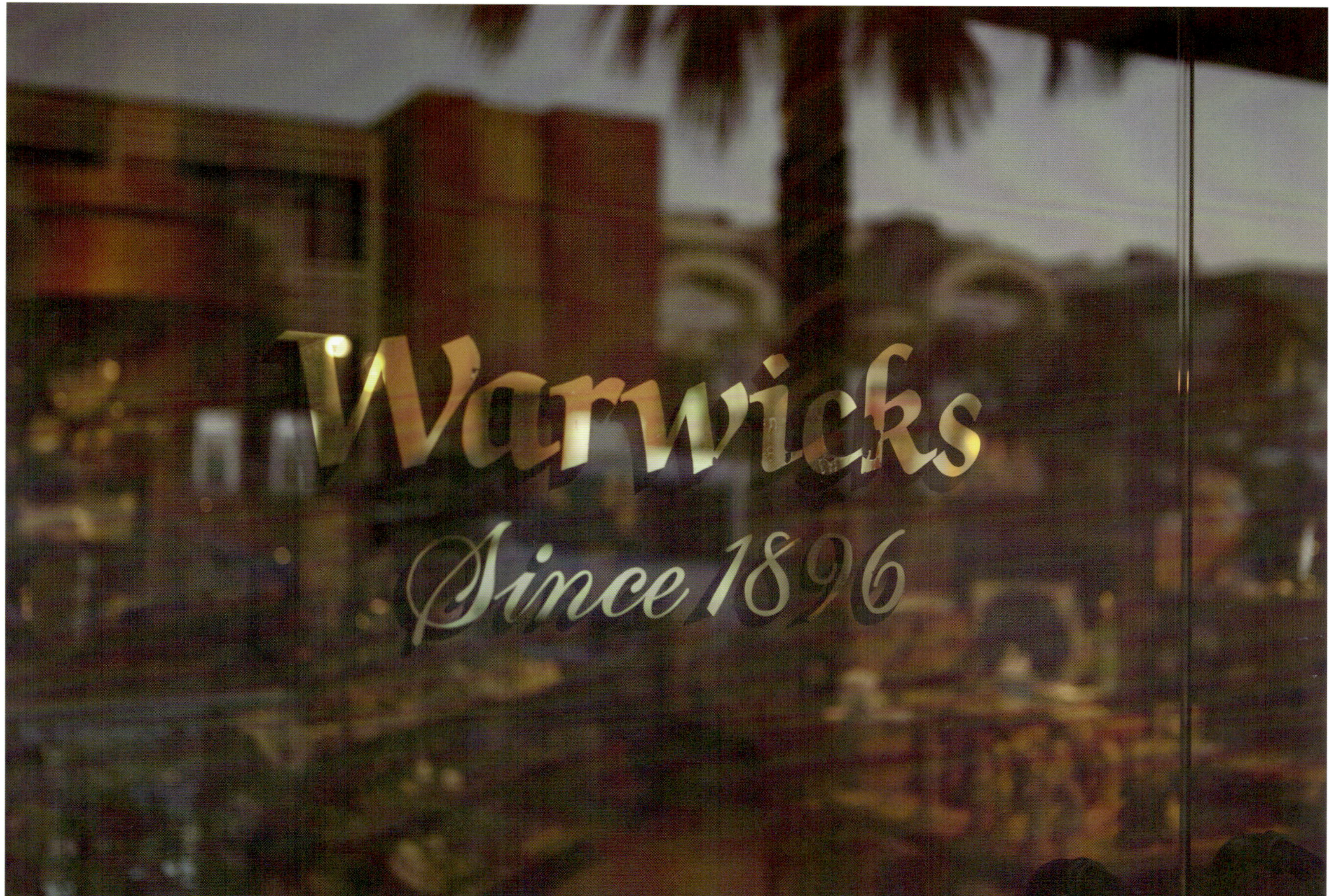

Warwicks
Since 1896

This is a place where sunshine, rare but stormy rain, fog, and chilling winds take turns shaping the atmosphere of the day. A place where the position of the sun, the moon, or the stars always seems out of the ordinary. The ocean is very near down these daunting white cliffs and you can feel its mysterious, inspiring and salty presence in the air, although it remains mostly silent. This is the land of the Torrey Pine trees, remnants of a prehistoric mountain range now submerged in the Pacific Ocean. Rare and tall, they are found in the wild almost exclusively along this local stretch of coastline in San Diego County. But for most visitors, the trees are merely a backdrop to the main event. Because, when all is said and done, this is a place where people come from all over the continent and beyond to play golf.

Down on the beach below this extraordinary area, naked men and women (but mostly naked men) stretch out for full-body tans on warm sunny days. In recent decades, the proximity of these rare and enigmatic trees has compelled modern men to act in odd and ingenious ways. The

stunning site was bought on the eve of the Second World War by the military, which then used it as an anti-aircraft artillery training center and built a city of 15,000 souls around it in only a few months, complete with paved streets and nearly 300 buildings, including three theaters and five chapels. They abandoned it as soon as the war ended and the site was then used as a racecourse for some time. But before long men changed their minds again: they decided to design and build a golf course in its place.

Not your average golf course, mind you. "With a name that stirs the imagination of golf enthusiasts all over the world, and the many holes on both the North and South courses that provide dramatic ocean views, Torrey Pines Municipal Golf Course is often referred to as 'Pebble Beach South' and is truly a golfer's paradise," stress the spirited brochures. Playing at Hole #6, Torrey Pines Golf Course's "signature hole" with a tremendous change in elevation, seems to be the ultimate golfer's fantasy. While relaxing before a decisive play, you can meditate on the rugged ocean cliffs for a

minute or so, catching a glimpse now and then of dolphins playing in the waves, or gliders flying over the unusual treetops.

Men are not allowed to cut down Torrey Pine trees. Thus, being as they were in dire need of space to design their legendary golf course, they delicately relocated some of the trees to a different area of the course, and the trees survived. As if in tribute to the final masterpiece, when the US Golf Open rolls around here, as in 2008, everything and everybody in the vicinity is sucked into a vortex of hysteria. The prices of all the rooms in the surrounding hotels suddenly double or triple. They fill up anyway, and very quickly too. Even on regular weekends, when Tiger Woods and other icons of the sport have returned to distant TV screens, people remain more eager to play golf at Torrey Pines than any of the more than 80 other golf courses scattered throughout San Diego County. Some are so enthusiastic that they get in line at 6 p.m. to play the following morning, dreaming of a course touched by dawn and shrouded in the magic attraction of the Torrey Pine trees.

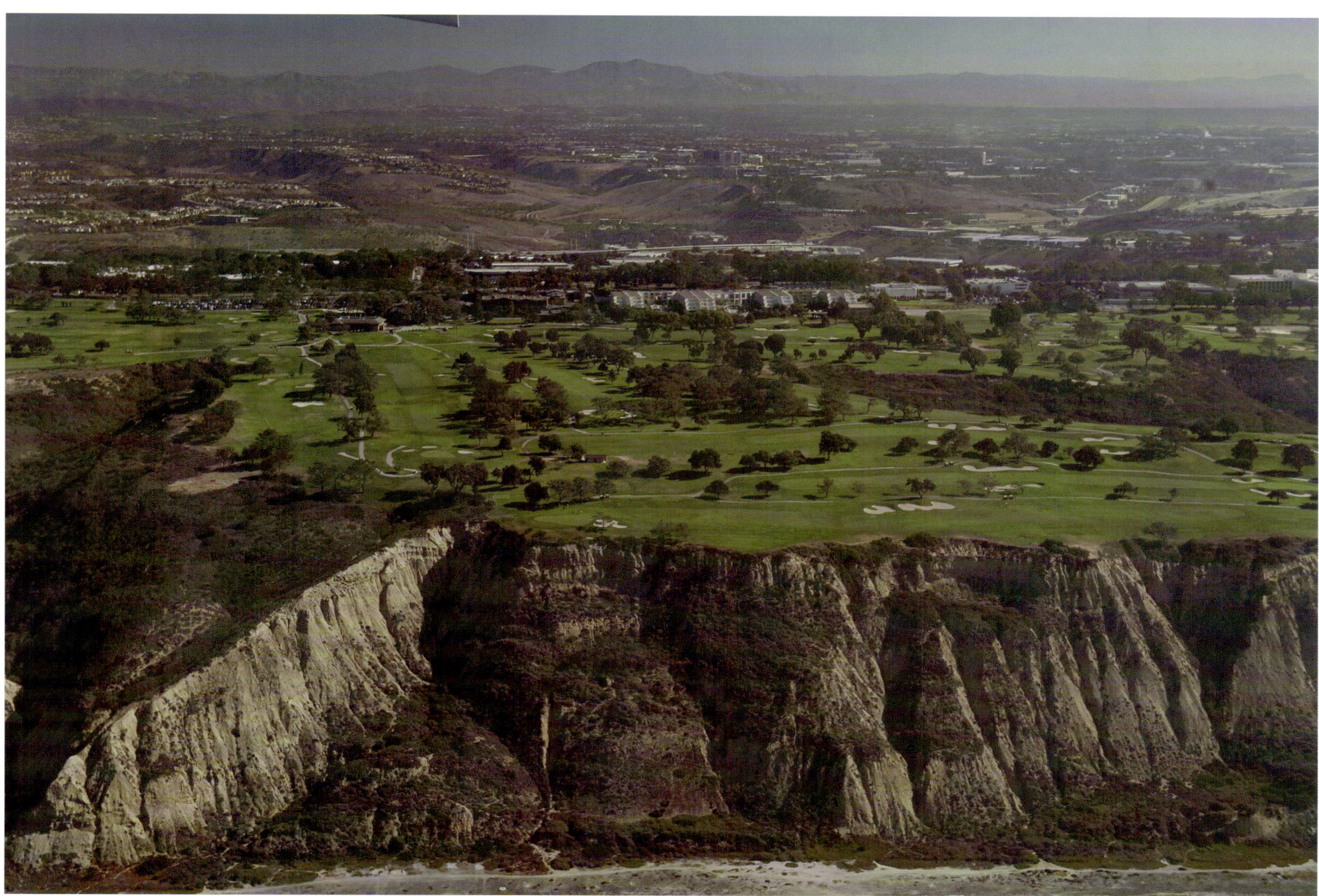

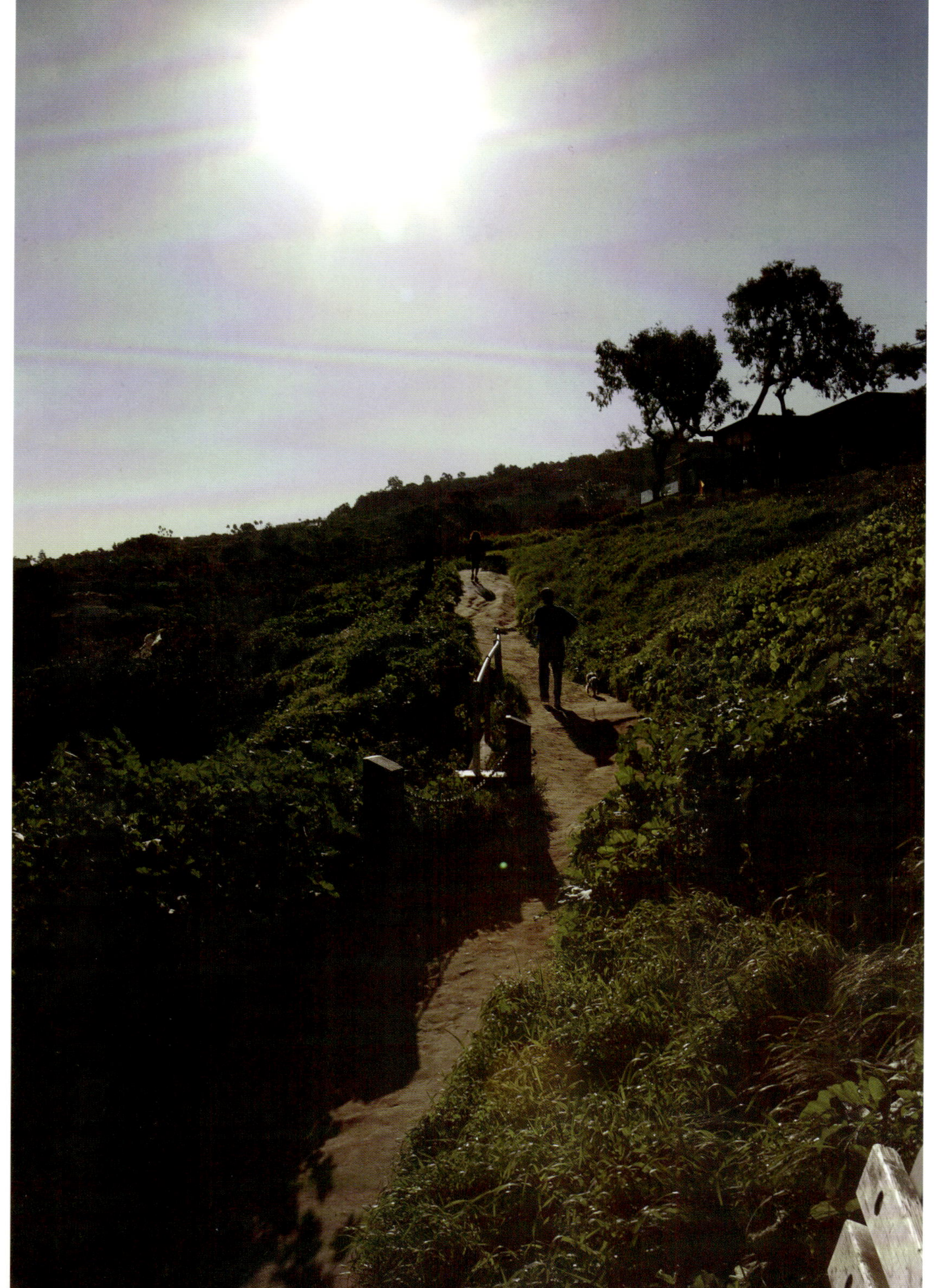

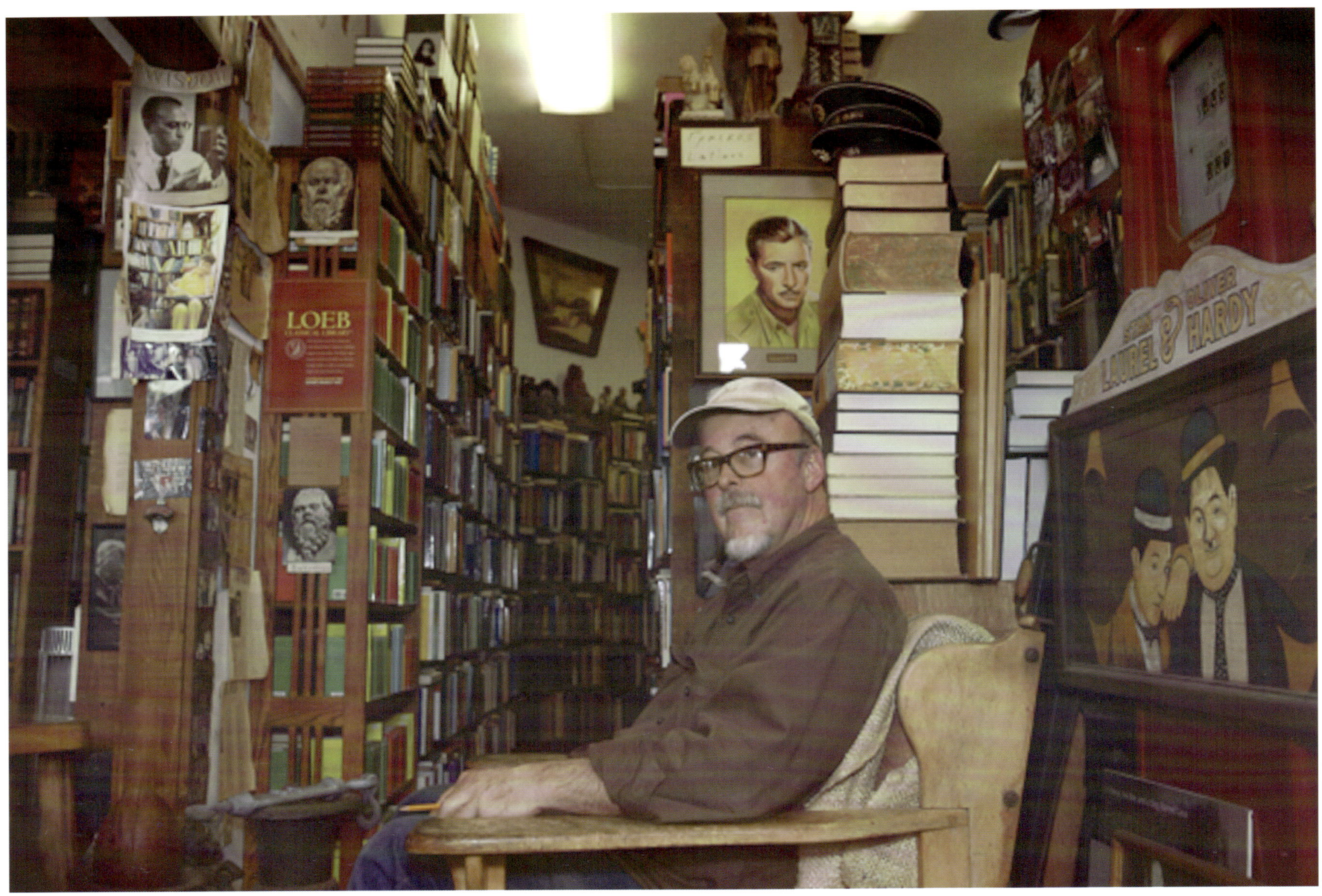

La Jolla is home to two main sorts of people, says Dennis Wills, owner of D.G.Wills Books: "It's a combination of wealthy Republicans and the educated community, living side by side." Dennis Wills has clearly chosen his side. "If it hadn't been for the university, I would have settled in Berkeley," he says, surrounded by thousands of books, old and new, at his store on Girard Avenue, right next to the Pannikin and the Ferrari dealer.

It's March, and there's a Debussy tune playing somewhere overhead. Scholars and UCSD professors wander the aisles in search of an old copy of Hegel or a novel they couldn't find anywhere else. No one is manning the counter. Dennis himself is outside, holding a glass of wine and chatting with friends. It's the same feeling you get in an old bookstore in Paris or London, the feeling that you can spend hours here without spending a dime, that it's okay to just talk with the owner about anything you like, and nobody's going to get mad at you. And Dennis has plenty to talk about. Straight out of his job decrypting Soviet pilot messages in the Air Force, Dennis arrived in La Jolla in 1979. He immediately opened a bookstore on La Jolla Boulevard. Passionate about his work, he made sure that his shop was open from 10 a.m. to 10 p.m. every day, including Sundays. It wasn't long before he started organizing events, hundreds of them, hosting the likes of everyone from Norman Mailer to Mike Davis. He proudly notes that his bookstore is one of the very few in the country to have hosted 5 of the legendary beat poets: Allen Ginsberg, Gary Snyder, Michael McClure, Lawrence Ferlinghetti, and Ted Joans. He tracked them down all the way from New York to San Francisco to invite them to come and talk right here in La Jolla.

It's a late summer evening now and there's a black and white silent movie playing on the screen of an old television. A couple of friends are watching with Dennis, sipping red wine, entranced by the riveting eyes of a long-dead German actress. Another of Dennis' passions is for expressionist movies of the twenties. Pabst, Fritz Lang, Murnau. It's become tradition here to watch one of these legendary films at the end of the day, as customers continue to roam the now dark and mysterious aisles of the bookshop. Dennis would love to have Robert Osborne, the host of Turner Classic Movies, come here one day and talk about silent movies. "Actually, he doesn't know that... yet," he confesses with a smile, "but I'm going to write him a letter." More than 30 years after opening his first bookstore, there's little doubt that Dennis Wills is still passionate, and open seven days a week.

On Silverado Road in front of the village's traditional "cobbler," surrounded by modern buildings, banks, gyms and international clothing boutiques, the small Brick and Bell Café attracts a good number of people who live or work in the area. They come for the local atmosphere, the charm of this little brick house with a bell hanging from its façade, the extended open hours and, of course, the Colombian coffee. But most of all, according to its owner, Peter Schumacher, they come for the scones.

These increasingly famous pastries come large and small, in cranberry, blueberry, apple cinnamon and chocolate chip flavors, and this morning there's no shortage of customers lining up for them. The lines keep Peter's employees, all of whom come from places with evocative names like Porto Alegre or Florianópolis in Brazil, on their toes. The room is filled with the smell of coffee grains left to dry on the counter and of the scones and pastries which Peter himself baked at dawn. Waiting for their turn to order, wealthy business people and retirees exchange thoughts about how beautiful the day already is with a coastal California smile. Two much simpler-looking women exchange fewer words in Spanish. What Peter is most proud of, he says, is the fact that people from all social and cultural backgrounds, including celebrities (but that's a secret), come to the Brick and Bell. They wait side by side in line together for their morning coffee, and all of them feel comfortable.

Peter Schumacher himself came to the US from Germany in the eighties. Originally from Leipzig, he used to work as a coach for the German soccer team Schalke 04 and decided to come to La Jolla after he got a job as a soccer coach. If Peter's Brick and Bell Café is now among the three busiest independent cafés in San Diego at a location where three previous cafés have failed, that's because, he insists with a suddenly thicker German accent, "they used to get here at 7:30. But you need to arrive at four in the morning if you want to succeed!"

These days, the Brick and Bell opens before dawn, around 4 a.m., to serve strong coffee to bankers who wake up long before Wall Street opens in New York. The flood gates really open at 6:30, and the stream of diverse patrons doesn't slow until early afternoon. Some days the café's eight Brazilian employees serve up to 1,000 customers, and in a year, Peter says, they go through about 7,500 pounds of coffee and 40,000 pounds of milk. But the real record is for the Brick and Bell scone. In the year 2008 alone, Peter sold about 70,000 of them. Some people surely had more than one.

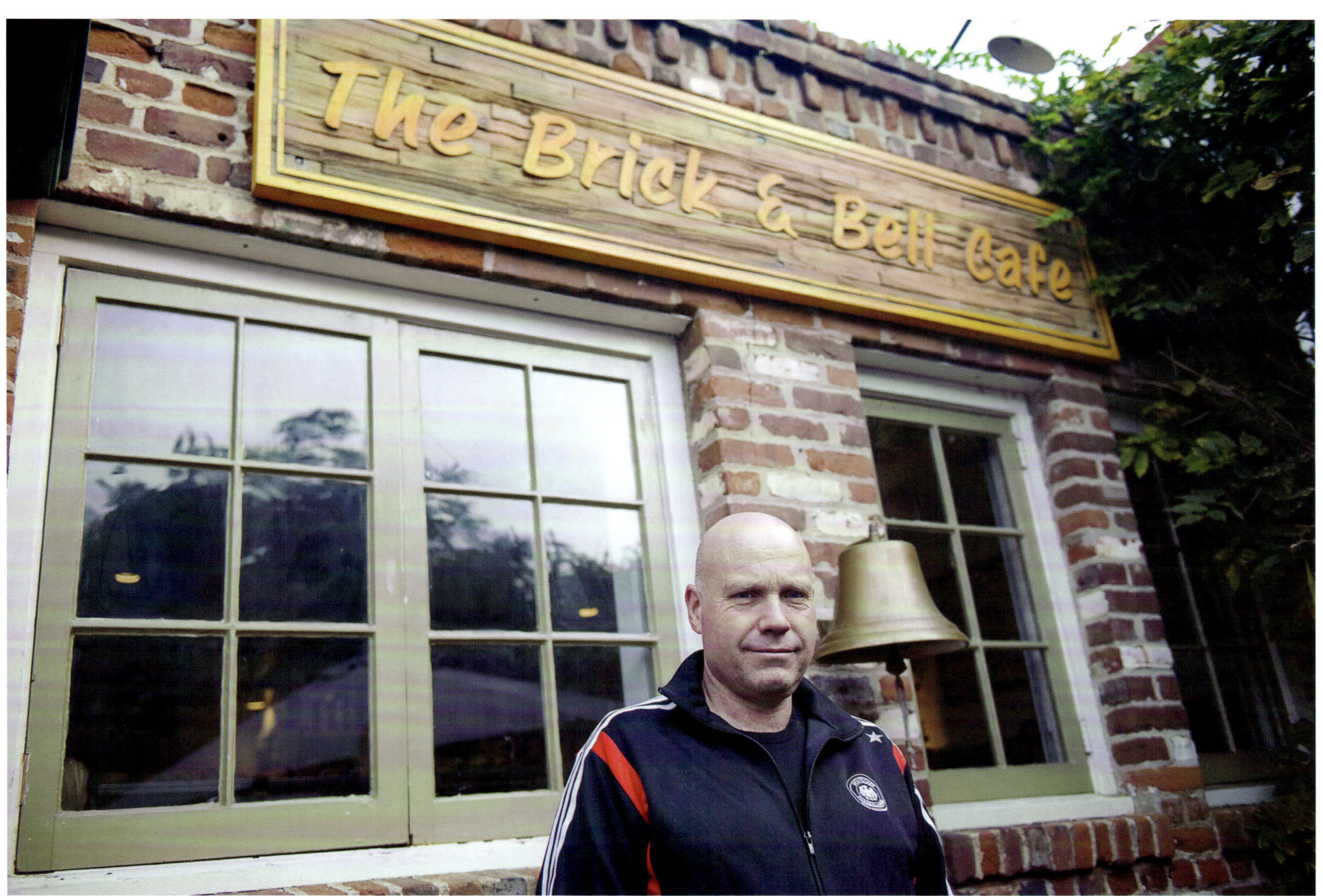

The Brick & Bell Cafe

In 1888, there were only 11 buildings in La Jolla: a hotel, some hotel cotages, and a few houses. However, this did not last long. By 1939, 1,199 houses had been built. Most houses were built in the 70's: 6,080 of them, compared to 3,444 in the 50's. More recently, the 90's witnessed the construction of 1,851 new homes. All told, there are 19,539 combined houses and condos in La Jolla today. By contrast, there are only 6,894 apartments.

There is a noticeable scarcity of high-rise buildings in the area, which is one of the charms of La Jolla's coastline. On average, a standard La Jolla house contains 6 rooms, and an average apartment has between 3 to 4 rooms; most of the houses have 3 bedrooms, but 1,182 of them have 5 or more. However, most of the apartments contain only 2 bedrooms.

From the outside, it looks like an opaque fortress, at once modern and vaguely reminiscent of times before antiquity. Five concrete towers devoid of any openings line it on each side. Arrive there in the morning and the whole edifice is surrounded by thin layers of marine fog, moving toward it and then disappearing again somewhere along the way. Are we about to enter the secretive Temple of Science?

On the contrary, despite its guarded-looking exterior, The Salk Institute is open to any wandering soul. Or at least its courtyard is, paved with antique marble that looks as though it's been here for centuries. Stepping into it you find your-self flanked by two imposing, symmetrical, rectangular buildings that never fail to impress visitors of all kinds. A thin water channel carved through the travertine marble leads to a perfectly shaped basin, then into a splashing fountain that seems to end in the ocean. Or, on mornings like this, into a misty vision of infinity. *There are*

no *boundaries to human endeavor*, utters the water, carousing with abandon at the end of the neo-antique fountain. To the open imagination, it really might look like an offering to the Gods of Science.

Wandering around the aisles and corridors of the Institute, you can catch glimpses of the endless activity inside. Through giant glass panels you meet the eyes of a slighly startled researcher or a weary professor lost amongst a mess of computers, books, microscopes and test tubes, only to find yourself surrounded by silence and the strangeness of the whole place again a moment later. Louis Kahn designed the Institute according to Jonas Salk's wish that its mysterious and profound nature might inspire creativity among researchers and scientists. Salk himself was convinced that he found the inspiration to develop the polio vaccine in the contemplation of Assisi, Italy. These days, as if to prove his point, the Salk Institute counts *3* living Nobel laureates among its scientific staff for outstanding achievements in the fields of

brain hormone research, genetics and molecular biology, and cancer research.

Nevertheless, you can't help but notice the effect of time here and there, the deteriorating concrete maybe, or some exposed joints. Was it designed that way on purpose to contrast the buildings' ephemeral nature with that of the eternal flow of the water? In the marbled courtyard, tiny humans play gracefully around the imposing basin, jumping around like agile little spirits. A thicker layer of marine air suddenly refreshes the atmosphere. On the egress of a nearby dark corridor lies the light of day, saturated with fog. A giant squared mouth inside the concrete cube seems to swallow the clouds, and the sun is slowly emerging.

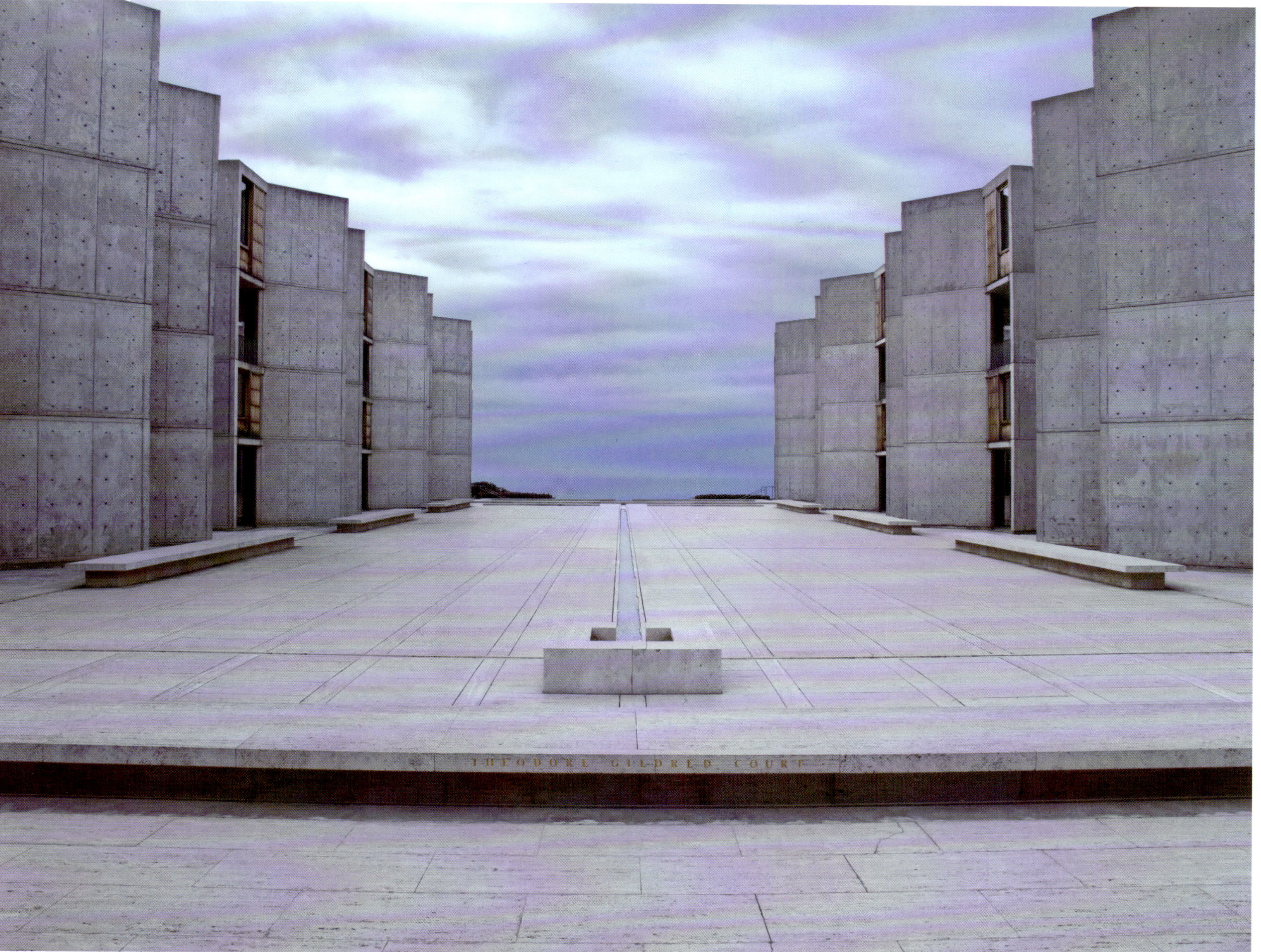

THEODORE GILDRED COURT

It's Sunday afternoon and Jonathan Segal is sitting on a *Papa Bear* chair designed by Hans Wegner, sipping a glass of wine. His wife Wendy is moving around the rest of the intimidating furniture with ease and style. They still live in this gorgeous house in the village, a house that was once a gas station and then a vacant lot that nobody really wanted. A house they designed and built entirely in 10 months. Still, but not for long.

The house is located only a couple of blocks away from where everything is going on. Everything, which is to say not much. Wendy and Jon have loved it here: it's been so peaceful and quiet, and so pretty. They could walk everywhere. But they also missed the diversity, the action you find in a big city and one day, they always said to each other, one day they might just leave. No matter how much they cherish this stunning house where every detail, every little piece of furniture has its importance. Jonathan insists on using the term "Modern" to describe it. "Modern, not contemporary," he emphasizes.

Jon grew up in Manhattan Beach, and Wendy is from Idaho. They recently celebrated their 25th wedding anniversary and have been in San Diego for just as many years. While their two kids, Matthew and Brittany, both in their early twenties, have already left San Diego, their 2 dogs Coco and Betty are still running wildly around the house. As for their two cats and their two bunny-rabbits, they're always hiding elsewhere in some of the house's more remote nooks and crannies. Both very gifted and successful architects, Wendy and Jon are used to working together. So far they have built and designed no fewer than 19 buildings in San Diego.

The move is happening so fast that they're still in shock. Despite their attachment to this house in the village, they're relocating downtown, where more things are happening, and happening faster. Wendy will soon be starting her wine bistro in Little Italy. Meanwhile, a successful and well-known couple from New York will be moving into the "Prospect house." They loved it so much when they visited that they decided to buy it right away, complete with all the furniture and they left the original design wholly intact. They now own one of the most beautiful residential buildings in La Jolla, a three-story wood-frame edifice surrounded by a reflecting pool on one side and a glass floor on the opposite, built and designed in ten months by two of the most ingenious architects in California.

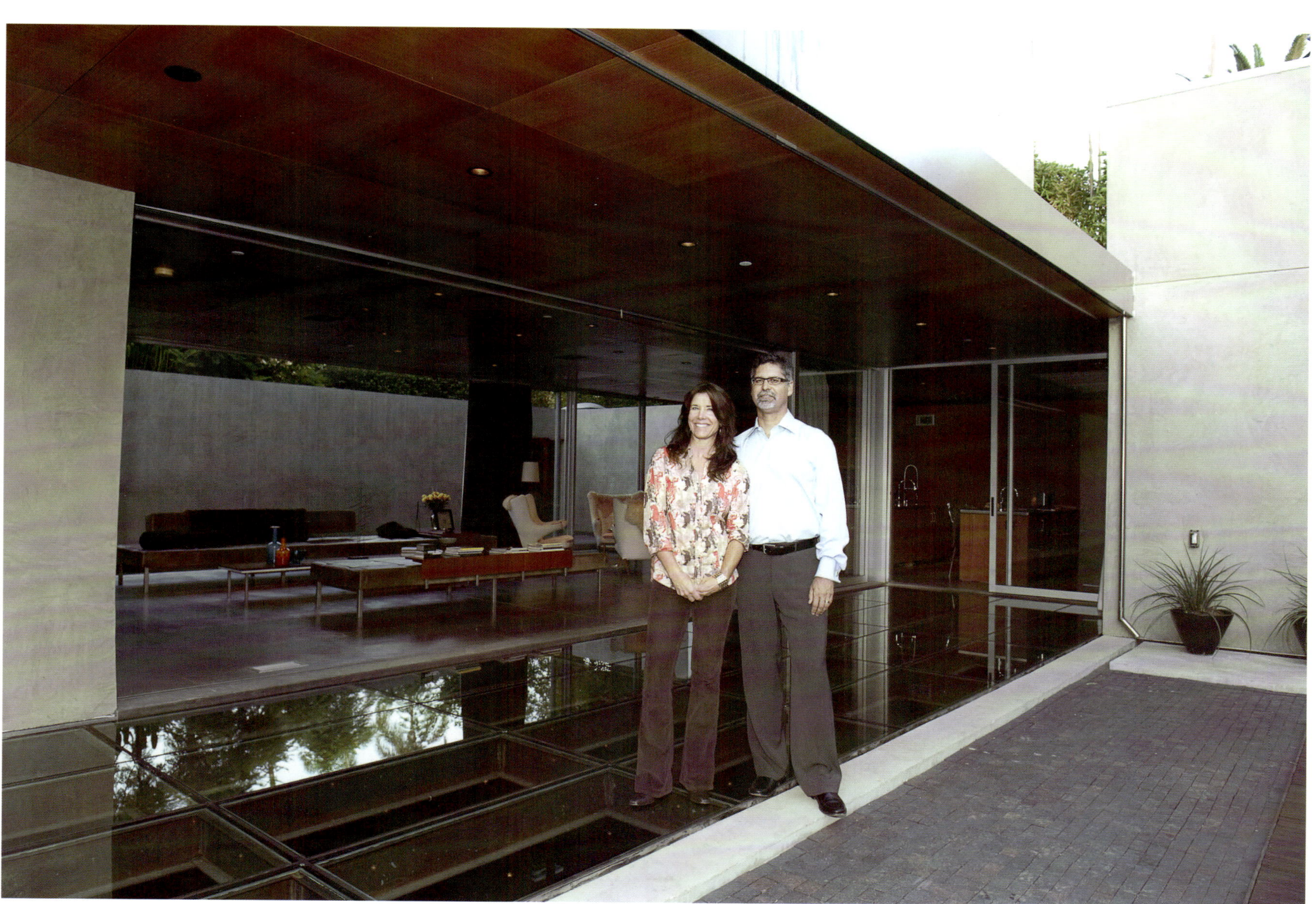

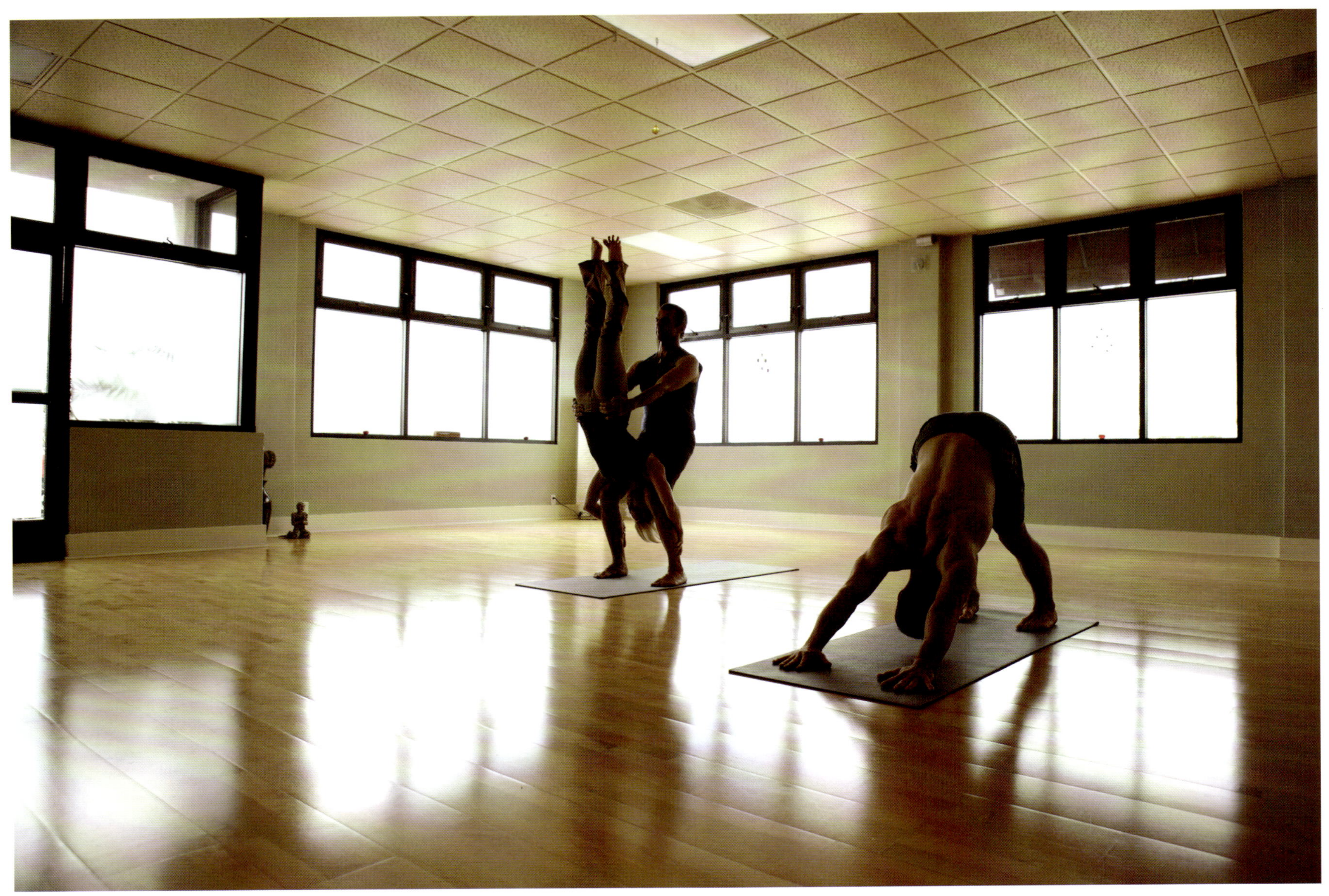

Gerhard, Amy Jo and Roman practicing at Prana
Yoga Center on Silverado Street.

The stage has been set for a long, long time, and it's awfully beautiful. Rigid cliffs on both sides and the gentle hills behind them enclose a large stretch of fine sand. A good crowd of individuals of all sizes is gathering to enjoy the last moments of the day, and the first whispers of the night. Dark clouds are gathering too, building on the horizon as if to warn of an approaching tempest. But everybody knows it's not going to happen. It's only the illusion of a storm, a well-intentioned aesthetic treat to break the monotony of the strange sense of tedium that paradise, with its exhausting glut of beauty, brings.

You breathe deeply; even close your eyes. You listen to the waves crashing softly onto the sand and fatigue starts to fade away. You listen to human voices throwing words at the endless horizon in a jumble of world languages: English, Spanish, and Russian... Arabic or Farsi... Tagalog, Mandarin and Japanese. Walking on the beach of La Jolla Shores, the profusion of sounds, of sights, of smells, the rare sense of true diversity,

transports you. Emerging from the ocean, 1 ageless surfer forgets to watch where he's going, missing you by inches. Joggers in shorts, veiled middle-eastern women, silent dreamers and dressed up couples on their way to a party or restaurant drift past. Some argue bitterly, others kiss repeatedly, but as the night approaches and the colors become more dramatic, each of them turns into a dark and pulsating silhouette, their features indistinct.

Getting closer to the Pacific Ocean, a few solitary individuals gaze at the Cove on the other side, watching its stiff hills covered in wealthy villas slowly turning into a collection of tiny electric lights, content to leave their feet in the pleasurably cold water. Overhead, seagulls are laughing at each other and everything around, mocking the cycle of days and all this inexplicable beauty. The distant screams of Latino kids playing soccer on the beach hover beneath their cacophony. A bitter-sweet darkness is descending on the scene now, and even the silhouettes begin to

vanish into waiting cars or hotels. Your own schedule comes flooding back from the place where life had been suspended, and you're ready to leave. For a moment, the sunset on La Jolla Shores had an absorbing power that San Diego often lacks. Something that let you connect with a wider humanity. Something like the true feel of a big city.

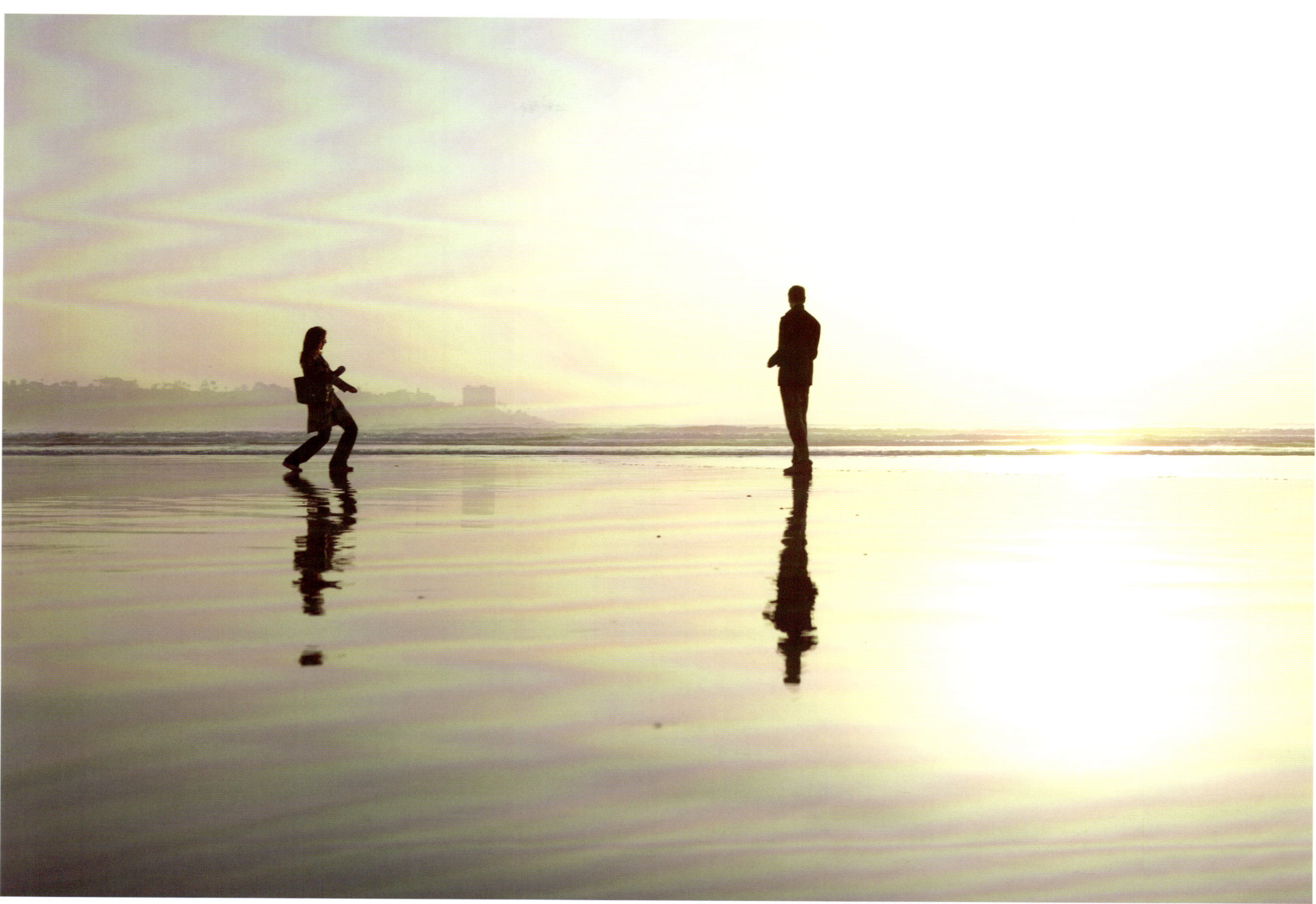

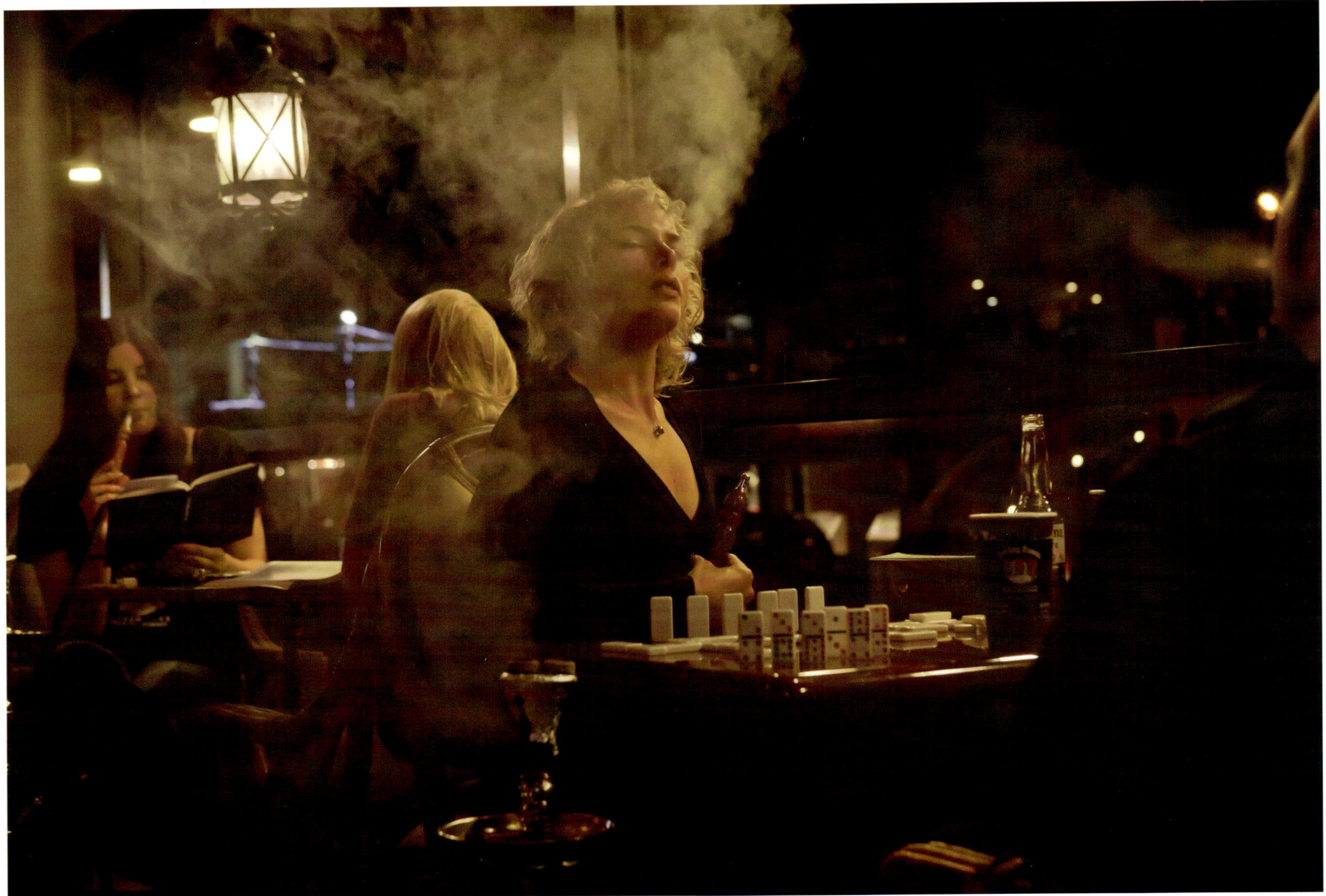

Smoking hookah in the Living Room Café at the intersection
of Prospect Street and Girard Avenue.

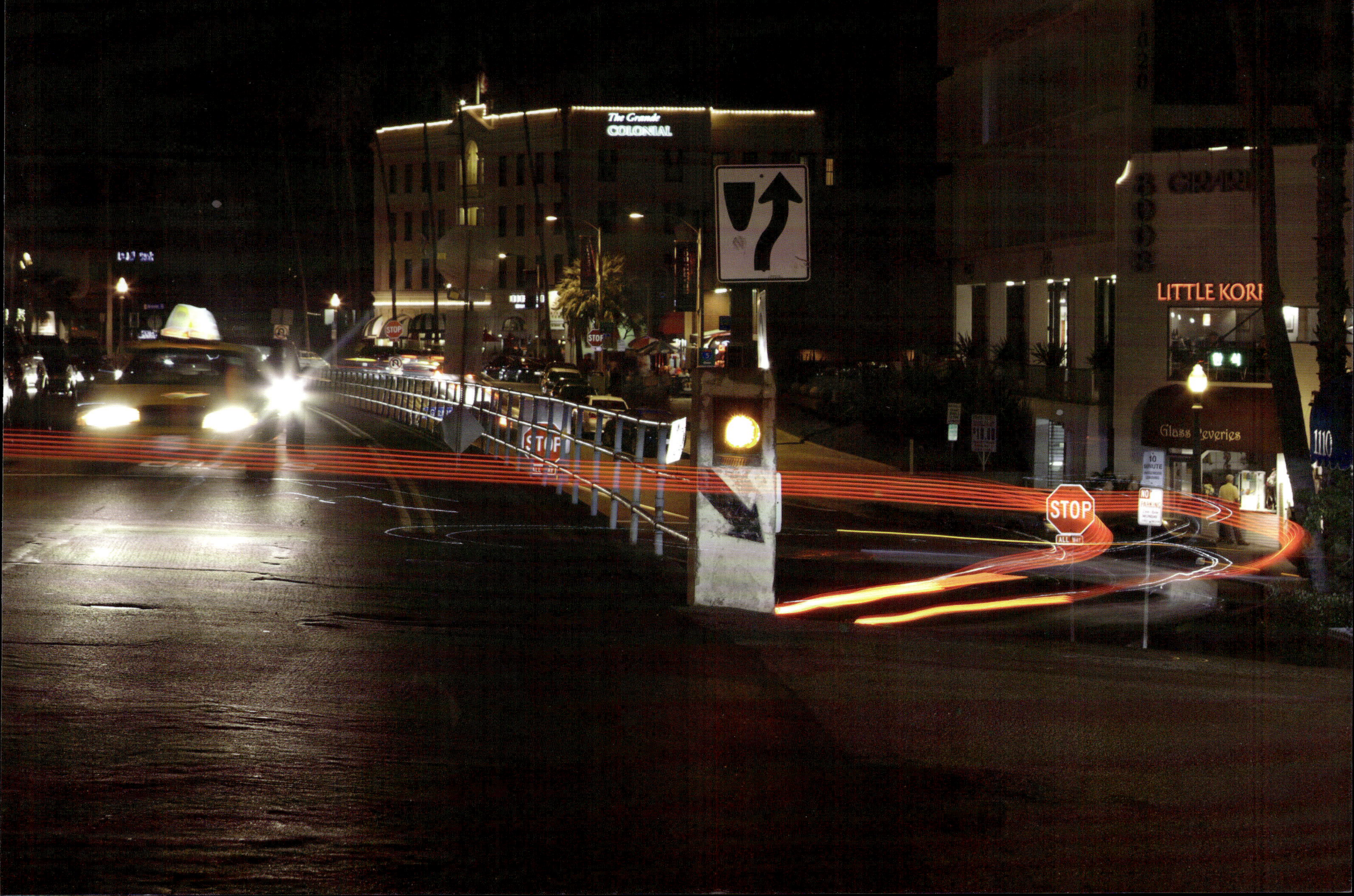
The Grande
COLONIAL
LITTLE KORE
Glass Reveries
STOP
ALL WAY
STOP
ALL WAY
STOP
STOP
10
MINUTE
1110

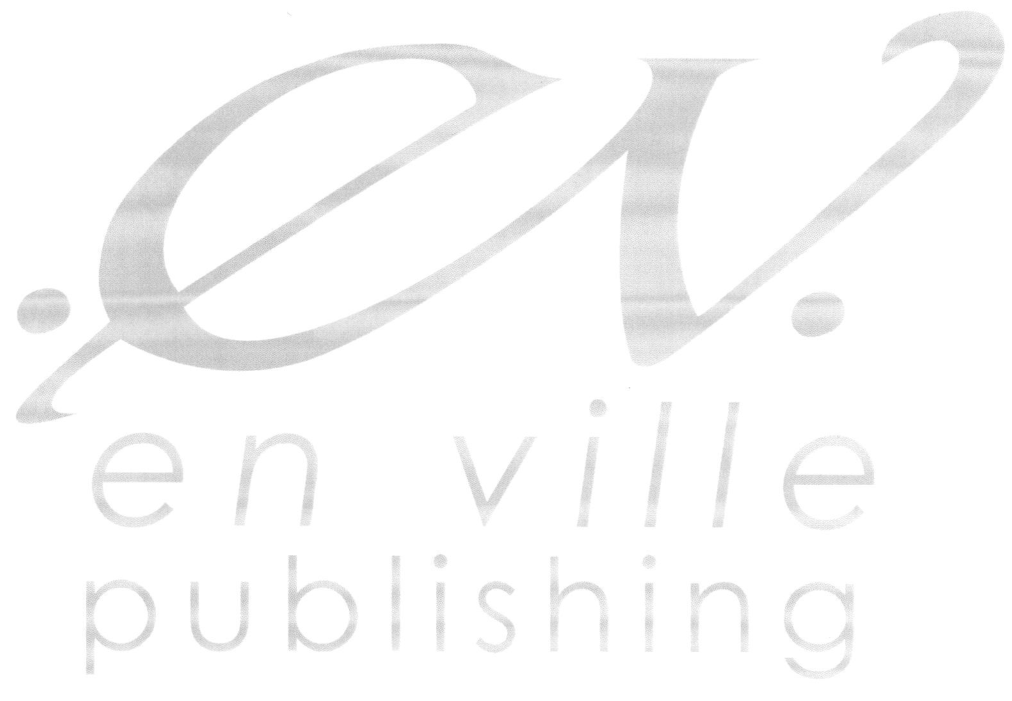
en ville
publishing

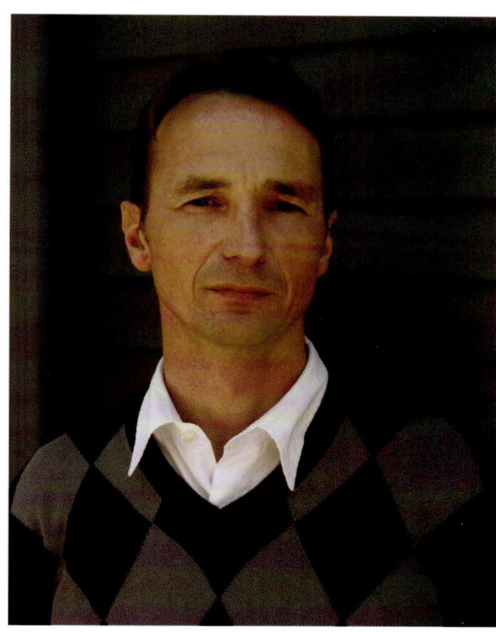

Olivier Dalle

Olivier moved to La Jolla from Paris seven years ago and is currently working as a French professor at Palomar College in San Marcos. Aside from teaching his native language, he has always been interested in traveling and writing. He spent four years in the Middle East and has published several books about Cairo and Beirut, focusing on culture and local life instead of tourist sites. He then relocated to the UK and traveled extensively in Africa, Brazil and Asia before finally arriving in the US, where he worked for a non-profit organization dedicated to staging contemporary art exhibitions in Washington DC. After a brief return to France, Olivier settled in California with his wife Aline, where he was quickly inspired to create a new collection of books focused on the diverse local communities of San Diego County.

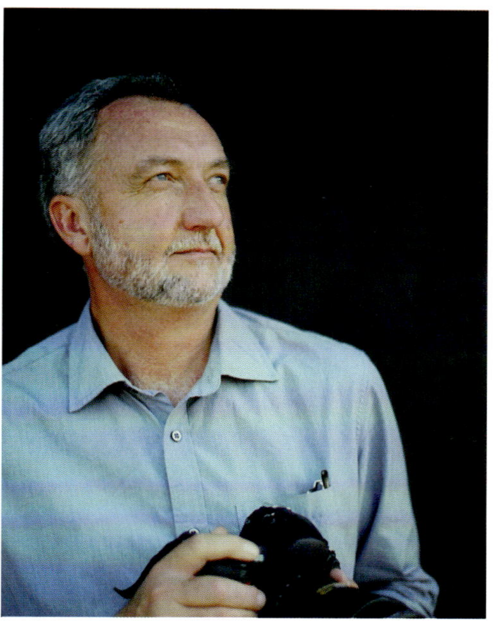

Paul Burlingame

Paul's passion for creating imagery started 30 years ago in the field of film photography. Other artistic pursuits have included the line drawing of faces on annual trips to Europe over a period of 10 years, pottery, figure painting, and, for the past several years, photographing people on a weekly basis. He opened a studio and started his own photography company in 2007 (www.paulburlingamephoto.com). Paul is inspired by fashion (especially European magazines such as Vogue Italia), modern music, furniture and paintings. A native of Boulder, Colorado, Paul has lived in La Jolla for five years and in the San Diego area for the past 12 years. His work has been shown at a variety of locations including Amsterdam, display windows for vintage dress shops in San Diego, and at the Linkery Restaurant in North Park.

Editor   Kristine Serio
Designer   Sabrina Sullivan
Printing Manager Lu Chao

We would like to deeply thank our sponsors, who believed in the book long before it was published. Their contributions have made the book possible and proven them to be true local partners in the community, supporting unique cultural endeavors.

Very Special Thanks to:

Warwick's
Peter at the Brick and Bell Café

The Grande Colonial Hotel
Louis Zalesjak at Maître D' restaurant
Aja Rugs

La Valencia Hotel
Meg Lebastchi at Coldwell Banker
Wendy and Jonathan Segal
Ross Thiele & Son
Gerhard at Prana Yoga Center

We would like to thank all those who have supported and helped us in the three years it took us to create this book. Thanks for believing in the project, introducing us to the right people, pointing us in the right direction, telling us all the cool anecdotes about La Jolla and even committing to buy some books.

Thanks again to: Elyse Baktis; Anita Busquets and Bill Ladd; Jean-Michel, Sylvie and Ludo at Tapenade restaurant; Farnaz and Axel at Serenity Shoe Boutique; James Alcorn; Sandy Mc Creight; Enzo at La Dolce Vita; Mary Cook at La Jolla Playhouse; Marie-Claude and Stéphane Dalle; Nasrine at Sahel Bazaar; John Fish, Gary Rosenberg and Jim Nelson at Score; Leah and Craig; Betty Loria; Svetlana and Maurizio Zanetti; Alix Stecker; Paola Gonzales; Rita Furlong; Chris Bowers; Sabine at the Tourist Office; Christine Spindler; John Mc Nutt; Susan Spencer; Brandon Holmes; Joanne Randolphe; Glenda Lynne; Laure and Tristan Grimbert; Sandrine and Franck Danglard; Eron Tarail; Judith Fauconnier; Aline Thiébaut.

Credits

Most statistics about the zip code 92037 have been researched at:

http://www.city-data.com

Photograph next to the World Map by Marissa Parsons.

Photograph for the Niki de Saint Phalle page:

Work visible in the image:

Niki de Saint Phalle
Big Ganesh, 1998 steel, polystyrene foam, polyurethane, automotive paint, electronic component, light bulbs,
and iron base elephant: 128 x 62 x 58 in. (325.1 x 157.5 x 147.3 cm); mouse: 26 x 18 x 15 in. (66.0 x 71.1 x 38.1 cm)
Collection: Museum of Contemporary Art San Diego
Gift of Ron and Mary Taylor to honor Martha Longenecker, Founder, Mingei International Museum of Folk Art

Photograph of the Museum of Contemporary Art:

Architecture:

Originally an Irving Gill-designed residence, Venturi, Scott Brown & Associates' renovated the MCASD La Jolla location in 1996.

Works visible in the image:

Nancy Rubins
Pleasure Point, 2006 nautical vessels, stainless steel, stainless steel wire 304 x 637 x 288 in. (772.2 x 1618 x 731.5 cm)
Collection: Museum of Contemporary Art San Diego
Museum purchase, International and Contemporary Collectors Funds

Ed Ruscha
Brave Men of La Jolla, 1995-1996 acrylic on PVC coated fabric 24.75 x 36 feet (7.5 x 11 meters)
Collection: Museum of Contemporary Art San Diego
Museum purchase with proceeds from the Museum of Contemporary Art San Diego Art Auction 2006 and from prior donations
by Susan and Frank Kockritz and Mr. and Mrs. Norton S. Walbridge

Mauro Staccioli
Untitled, 1987 plywood, cement, red pigment, and metal 6. 2 feet x 29 feet x 11 in. (1.9 meters x 8.8 meters x 28 cm)
Collection: Museum of Contemporary Art San Diego
Extended loan by the artist

Judith Shea
Eden, 1987 bronze female figure: 55 1/2 x 15 x 9 in. (141.0 x 38.1 x 22.9 cm); male figure: 60 3/4 x 29 x 17 in. (154.3 x 73.7 x
43.2 cm)
Collection: Museum of Contemporary Art San Diego
Extended loan of Collette Carson and Dr. Ivor Royston

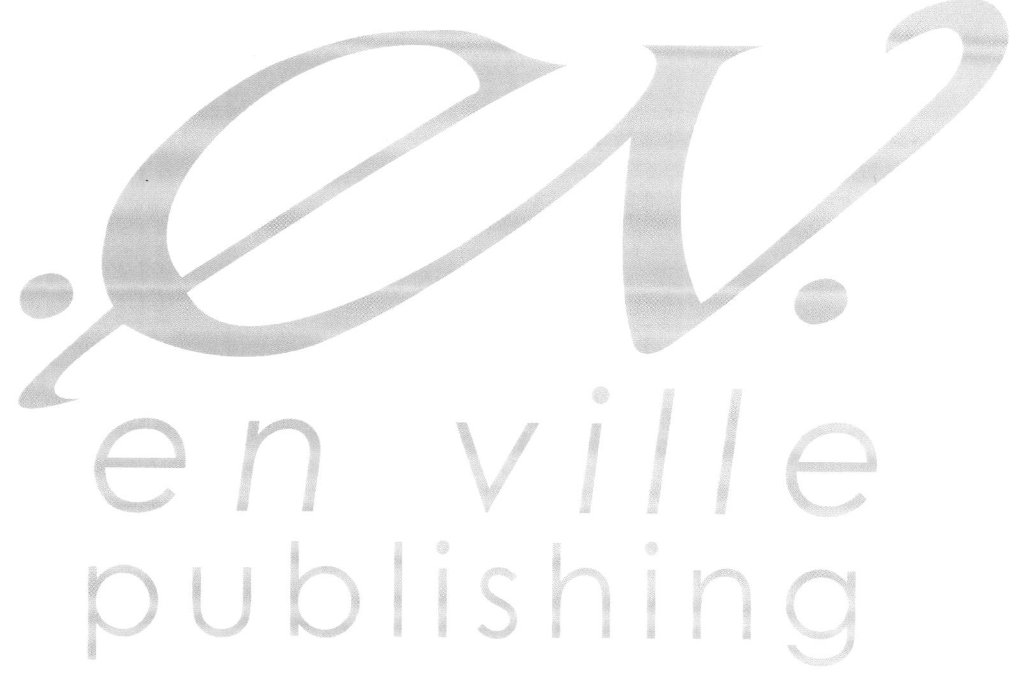